BOOK TITLE:

Top Secret keys to Wealth and Riches

Authored by Emmanuel Philippe

Preface:

They say if you want to be rich you should hang around rich people this advice sounds Reasonable. After all birds of a feather do flock together however this is only half the story if you really want to be rich you have to think and act like the rich here's 15 examples of how the reach think an egg so you can adopt a mentality before we get deeper into the book.

Example number one rich people think selfishness is a virtue average people feel they need to save the world and put others before themselves which is keeping them for rich people take the attitude that if they don't help themselves first they can't help anyone else.

Example number 2 rich people have an action mentality you want to see a rich person London up to play the lottery even before they were rich average people are always waiting on someone else to help them get rich such as a friend spouse the government even a lottery dependent on other people turn you to a beggar and keeps you poor rich people to take action and spend time solving problems.

Example number 3 rich people favorite specific knowledge of a formal education average people believe the road to riches is through doing masters and doctorate rich people are generally rich because they have made money selling a specific knowledge they have acquired many never even attended college

Example number 4 rich people dream of the future rich people spend a lot of time looking into the future setting goals and looking forward to what lies ahead average people dwell on the past which often holds them back by making them unhappy and depressed

Example number 5 rich people think about money logically average people and well educated people can fall into the trap of thinking about money emotionally and just wanting to retire comfortably rich people maintain a logical Tool that represents options and opportunities

Example number 6 rich people follow their passion rich people to find a way of getting paid for doing something they love average people earn money doing things they don't love

Example number 7 rich people aim high average people sit lower expectations to avoid disappointment whereas rich people set huge expectation and work hard to follow their dreams

Example number 8 which people believe you have to be someone average people on the other hand believe you have to do something to be rich and focus on immediate results rich people continuously focus on bettering themselves and learn from success and failures

Example number 9 rich people use other peoples money average people believed they need their own money to make money whereas rich people have no problem using other peoples money

Example number 10 rich people live the loader means rich people adapt the attitude of getting rich so they can afford to live by Lowder means average people live beyond their means instead of saving their money they spend it so that they can look rich

Example 11 rich people teach their children how to be rich average people taste your kids how to be good employees Whereas rich people teach their children about economics networking and how to be entrepreneurs

Example 12 rich people don't let money stress them out average people do rich people find peace of mind and wealth and I'm not afraid to admit that money can solve most problems allowing them to make more money average people see money as a continuous battle and necessary evil they have to endure average people have a poor relationship with money because they're always fighting to make it and keep it

Example 13 Rich people would rather be educated than entertained average people or opposite they read tabloids stay on social media and clubs rather than continuously educating them selves

Example 14 rich people surround themselves with like minded people average people think rich people are snobs so they develop a negative attitude towards the wealthy rich people steer clear of the doom and gloom attitude adding fuel to the fire of this snob label

Example 15 rich people focus on earning average people focus on sewing and miss big opportunities by trying to live frugally an average person rather spend money on a luxury car and designer before they spend on an investment rich people constantly focus on the big picture and how to earn the big bucks

Acknowledgement

First and foremost, I think the man who's watching from above God, who keeps on blessing me endlessly and continuously protect/preserve my life. God has brought me to my lowest level of existence to humble me, to add to my growth and development, and to shower me with wisdom, knowledge, and understanding. Because of God I was able to overcome, excel, achieve, and acquire all of what my heart desires, therefore all my praise and gratitude goes to the most high.

To my loving mother I thank you for being such a phenomenal/formidable woman, I know growing up I was a handful due to my rebellious nature. Still you never gave up on me, you were always a force to be reckoned with. I know most times I took you for granted and was unappreciative of things you've done for me, are you still never gave up on me I apologize for all the hard eggs I put you through. I know this new pair that shows will make you proud, I love you with all my being your truly a queen thank you times 1 million.

You know I have to save the best for last to my loving father who is also my best friend and better half, I don't even know where to start. The day me and the family got the call you were gone my life was in shambles, I became a puzzle with missing pieces that was impossible to put back together. By losing you I lost myself – you're dead traumatize me, I'm still hurt and in denial till this day.

You were and always will be my superhero, I know this new path and success will make you proud And keep a smile on your face. You were a great father who lead by example and lived a respectable life I will never forget you you always live on in my heart, thoughts, dreams, and blood that runs through my veins. I know you still here with me which is why I'm in the now, because I know for a fact superheroes don't know – I love you may you rest in paradise in peace until we see each other again.

TABLE OF CONTENT

Index of Definition

Business terms:

RFP– Request for proposal

CMS– Content management system

BBB – better business bureau

CRM – customer relationship management

INC – Inc.

SIC – standard industrial classification

CORP – corporation

LLC – limited liability company

LLP– Limited liability partnership

DDA – doing business as

SBA – small business association

IRS – Internal Revenue Service

EIN – employer identification number

TIN – tax identification number

AMT – annual minimum tax

LTD – limited

Financial terms:

IR a – individual retirement account

W – two – wages, salaries, tips etc.

SS-social Security

D&B – done in Broad Street newline INS – insurance newline LOC – line of credit newline OPM – other peoples money

INT – interest

P&L – profit and loss

NOL – net operating loss

COD – cash on delivery

1099 – self employed person or agent

POS – point of sale

Company Divisions:

MKTG – marketing

ACCT – accounting

AP – accounts payable

AR – accounts receivable

CR – credit

PR – public relations

HR – human resources

MIS –Management information

PRL – payroll

FIN – finance

GL – general ledger

Company Officers:

CEO – chief executive officer

CFO – chief financial officer

COO – chief operation officer

PR – president

VP – vice president

TR – treasurer

S EC – secretary

DIR – Director

MRGN Dash manager

DOS – Director of sales

CPA – certified public accountant

INTRODUCTION

The decision to to start a new business is yours to make. You have to jump in with both feet, you'll never succeed by having one foot in and one foot out it takes a very ambitious and strong minded/dedicated person to start a business.

This book you're about to read is filled with top-secret information and loopholes most people will never teach or reveal, they rather keep it in the family I chose in circle. I've dedicated endless hours of my time researching, reading, and interviewing some of the world greatest minds to finally dig up such a valuable information. I was fortunate enough to be in the midst of millionaires and billionaires who runs Fortune 500 companies, franchises, etc. Mostly everything I learned from them is in this book.

Now this book is short into the point, there won't be any pointless chatter and stories about how hard and expensive it is to establish and maintain the business. Most business books I read and a boring me to death, leaving me disappointed feeling robbed of my time and money. Most book covers and titles are deceiving, aren't you tired of reading books then having to walk away without obtaining the keys and knowledge you were looking for?

I'm here to tell you today forget about investors, forget about selling your car, forget about asking family and friends for a loan, lastly forget about taking the equity out of your house to find your business ventures. I will be showing you how to get $180,000 for free within 180 days - (6 months), After I show you how to get this free money I also school you on what to do with it how to acquire assets and how to start any business under the sun.

Before we get into the first chapter of this book, I would like to give you a little motivational speech to help you thrive and climb the ladder of success. Since you bought this book and already gave me an indication you're motivated and ambitious, but some people still need that little extra push to overcome two of life greatest obstacles, which is fear and self doubt.

Starting a new business is a major life change, all of the changes positive it can be stressful. Please open your mind and your eyes pay close attention to what you're reading, don't ever feel guilty about losing a friend I significant other during this process.

That means you've outgrown them and they'll only be an anchor around your ankles if you keep them around, friends and business never mix stay away from anybody who doesn't see your vision and try to taint your success.

Always remember every person in life is weird direct do it to the law of their being; The dots which they have built into their character have brought them to the position they stand in. People are anxious to improve their circumstances financially, but are unwilling to improve themselves; They therefore remain bound. You will only begin to achieve things when You've ceased to cry, wine and play victim, and continues to search within yourself for the heading truth which regulates your life.

As you with that you're mine to that regulating factor, you will cease to accuse others for the cause of your condition, and build yourself up in strong noble thoughts; never give up I'll let certain circumstances the Terrio path, start using those circumstances as aids to your growth and development, and as a means of discouraging the healing powers and possibilities within yourself.

Thoughts of doubt and fear never accomplish Anything, they only lead to failure. Motivation, dedication, and ambition ceases when doubt and fear creep in. Doubt and fear or enemies of your mindset you must annihilate them, or you'll never amount to nothing. A person who conquers doubt and fear has or will overcome failure, keep in mind your soul always attracts what is secretly harbors which can be things that you love and fear.

Always cherish your dreams and visions work hard to make it a reality, all great achievement was at first only a dream/vision. Your dreams and visions is a promise of what one day you'll become. Please don't become a victim to fear and doubt a victim to thoughtless and ignorant people who hate and chastise you on your success they are fools that only see the parent effects of things and not the end the working of the things themselves, dumb seeing you acquire wealth will say you gained it by luck or chance, and failed to see all the time, work, sweat, Tears and blood you put into achieve your position.

There is no such thing as handouts or Wish on/praying for wealth, a person doing just get with a parade or wished for– Only what they've justly earned.

Your wishes and prayers are only gratified and answered when they harmonize with your thoughts and actions. So what are you waiting for? If this book don't erase our fears and doubts out of your mind, by giving you all these valuable keys and top secret to success I don't know what will.

Stop procrastinating and wasting valuable time, there's 24 hours in a day that's 168 hours a week. Even if you work full-time eight hours a day five days a week there's still 16 hours left in the day 128 hours for the week, even if you work doubles 16 hours a day 80 hours a week there's still eight hours left in a day. That's 88 hours a week even if you go to the club you still have 80 hours left, so what's the excuse?

Chapter 1

Get incorporated

Getting Incorporated is the easiest thing you'll probably be doing throughout this whole process, the whole process is easy but incorporation is not that hard. I'll tell you from my experience I didn't do no paperwork to get my LLC up and running, all you have to do is go on legal zoom.com or incfile.com which is what I use I use ink file to apply for my LLCC.

Before you go on ink for what you wanna do is go to irs.gov and apply for the free EIN number, the whole process will take you about five minutes and it's free. After you completed disturb then you go to ink factor and it will cost you about $300-$400 to get incorporated, depending on the state you're in. I incorporated my business in Georgia so it only cost me close to $200.

The reason why I chose ink file, is because they are professionals and when it comes to doing business paperwork why not pay somebody who knows what they're doing so you don't make a mistake and get in trouble with the IRS later on and get audited. We're thankful they offer a bunch of options, the more options you need the more is it gonna cost you to incorporate your business. But for a simple LLC it shouldn't cost you no more than two to $300 from ink file.

You don't have to show up to North Secretary of State office or do anything everything will be done for you online, you will need your ID Social Security number, proof of address, two different proofs of identification and when you submit all the proper paperwork online they will send you your incorporation letters and everything you'll need to open up a business account and get the ball rolling.

Simple isn't it? Most business books you'll probably be 30 pages in and you'll still be confused about how to start an LLC but it's pretty simple. Just use those website and they will guide you through everything.

Chapter 2:

Website/Domain & Email

My business website is trap house publishing.com and I used godaddy.com to develop my website. go Daddy is simple and easy to use you can do it yourself, you don't even need to hire a developer or nothing like that if you have some time on your hands you can easily customize the website to your liking.

My business website is trap house publishing.com and I used godaddy.com to develop my website. go Daddy is simple and easy to use you can do it yourself, you don't even need to hire a developer or nothing like that if you have some time on your hands you can easily customize the website to your liking.

Depending on the business that you're starting and what you plan on selling, you might not even need to create your own website. Shopify also offers the same thing but in a different way it's like you're using their server as your own website to sell your products, and they charge you a fee and pay them monthly as you continue to use their server. It all depends if you want your own website or if you do not want to go through the headache of having to create one you could just use Shopify with their Pre-built templates as a website

Chapter 3:

Business Address

If you own your own property you do not want to lose your real address as the headquarters for your business, to avoid any litigation and losing your property to lawsuits or whatever the case is. If you rent and you don't own, you could use your address but still it's not safe because you want to have your business listed on 411, on yelp and stuff like that and I doubt anybody would want their physical address listed all over the Internet.

The best thing to do is to Google different companies that offers virtual addresses, a virtual address is basically a professional building that receives all your mail is in packages it's like a PO Box but with a physical address to make customers feel more comfortable you know because a lot of businesses that use PO Box end up being scammers and what not.

If you incorporate with ink file they will offer you the option which will cost you an extra $250 and after taxes and everything it will add up to $300 and change to get a Virtual address for your business. And just like a PO Box you will have to pay for it monthly.

Chapter 4:

$180k & A1 Credit

Since getting the money to start a business is the most imperative part, in this chapter I'll be showing you the top secret trick using 23 steps that's very easy to follow, also by doing the steps you'll help bullshit Phico score which is a no-brainer if you were someone with bad credit or no credit at all.

Step 1: Go to TD Bank and open a bank account with them this bank will be your primary bank. So the bank employee you would like to open a checking and savings account, you'll most likely need $25– $50 to open such account. After opening the account deposit $1000 into the account, make sure you split it up put $500 in the checking and $500 into the savings account equaling $1000 total

Step 2: After successfully opening a checking And savings account with your primary bank which will refer to as bank a, you must wait seven business days then go to the bank and ask for a savings loan using the 500 in your savings account as collateral for the loan.

Step 3: Take that $500 loan and go to a completely different bank, Bank of America for example, which will be bank B an open savings account with the $500 you just took from bank A do not open the check ins which is a savings account.

Since getting the money to start a business is the most imperative part, in this chapter I'll be showing you the top secret trick using 23 steps that's very easy to follow, also by doing the steps you'll help bullshit Phico score which is a no-brainer if you were someone with bad credit or no credit at all.

Step 1: Go to TD Bank and open a bank account with them this bank will be your primary bank. So the bank employee you would like to open a checking and savings account, you'll most likely need $25– $50 to open such account. After opening the account deposit $1000 into the account, make sure you split it up put $500 in the checking and $500 into the savings account equaling $1000 total

Step 2: After successfully opening a checking And savings account with your primary bank which will refer to as bank a, you must wait seven business days then go to the bank and ask for a savings loan using the 500 in your savings account as collateral for the loan.

Step 3: Take that $500 loan and go to a completely different bank, Bank of America for example, which will be bank B an open savings account with the $500 you just took from bank A do not open the check ins which is a savings account.

Step 4: Wait an additional seven business days to go back to bank B and ask for a savings loan in the amount of $500, since you'll be using the $500 that's already in your account as collateral (same step as before).

Step 5: Take the $500 loan you just borrow from the bank be in go to completely different bank let's see Chase Bank for example, to open your third and final savings account with the $500, Chase Bank will be Bank C.

Step 6: Wait in additional seven business days then go back to Banksy and ask for a saving loan and the amount of $500.

Step 7: Take the $500 loan you just got from Bank C, and deposit it into your primary bank checking account which is bank a which is the TD Bank account that you first open bringing the balance from $500-$1000

Step 8: wait an additional 9 to 10 days to complete a billing cycle and arrange automatic electronic transfers from bank a checking account, to pay each loan payment on the pre-arranged date when the loan was taken out. This is the easiest way to go about it rather than doing it manually by taking the funds out and depositing it yourself, the bank can do it for you automatically – always remember work smarter not harder.

Step 9: 30 days into the plan after setting up the automatic electronic transfers in bank eight apply for a visa credit card while you were there at TD Bank. Use bank B and bank C, Commercial cards and utility cards as references on the application for the visa credit card. Keep in mind all loans and credit cards have to be in positive standing in order to receive a fair interest rate.

Step 10: in a couple more weeks; You should receive the visa credit card. Depending on which bank you use as your primary bank, that's why I recommend TD Bank as an example since they issued cards on the spot the same day. The visa credit card should have a $5000 limit, because you have a $5000 overdraft protection which guarantees the credit there it will be paid in full.

Step 11: after you receive the visa credit card from bank A, Go to the bank B and apply for a MasterCard.Use the visa credit card from TD Bank as a reference, in the bank will issue a temporary master credit card with $2500 balance.

Step 12: Go to a different bank that services discover credit cards, and apply for a credit card using your Visa and MasterCard credit card as references in the bank will issue you a temporary card with $2500. You can also do this online by going to discover.com.

*Keep in mind the temporary cards will only have half of the total spending limit $2500, and you will receive the plastic card within two weeks with the full limit of $5000.

*Now you're halfway into completing this goal which is three months (90 days). You should know I have a visa credit card with a $5000 limit, a MasterCard with a $5000 limit, and a Discover credit card with a $5000 limit, you should also have two commercial cards (cards from Macy's, TJ Max, etc) with a $5000 limit each, and a utility gas card with a $500 limit. Do the math your $20,500 richer – but wait there's more.

Step 13: remember you have a $1000 balance in your primary bank checking account which is bank A,Now get a cash advance from your Visa credit card for the whole $5000 and deposit the $5000 into the bank A checking's account. Bank A checking account should be at $6000, minus 3 months of automatic loan payment on the three outstanding loans from the other banks.

*Every time your primary bank, bank A Checking account balance increases your overdraft protection increases so it's imperative to maintain and increase this account as often as possible. Your overdraft protection is now up from $2500 – $5000 to $10,000 – $12,500.

Step 14: Call and increase the limit on the master and discover credit cards to $10,000 each. since your overdraft protection and your primary account is $10,000-$12,500 you can call and increase your card to $10,000.

Step 15: Apply for an American Express credit card using all your bank accounts bank A, bank B, bank C,Commercial cards, utility card, Visa credit card, master credit card, and Discover credit cards as references under American Express credit card application.

*Be sure to verify with all of your banks, how often you'll be able to increase your limits on all the credit cards you have since this will be a key factor later on in this plan. Most banks allow monthly increases on credit cards, but depending on the persons credit ratings exception could be made.

Step 16: remember and step 13 you took a cash advance loan for $5000 from the Visa credit card to put into the bank a checking account. Now you use the MasterCard to pay off the Visa credit card, the MasterCard has a $10,000 balance use 5000 from the MasterCard to pay off the Visa card completely. Then call the Visa card and increase the limit on the Visa card to $10,000, leaving the MasterCard with $5000, The visa card should have $10,000, and the Discover card with $10,000.

Step 17: get a cash advance from your Discover card for $5000 and deposit that $5000 into the bank a check in the account bringing the balance to $11,000, and your overdraft protection will go from $10,000-$12,000 To $20,000-$25,000. Now we're 120 days into the plan, and your American Express card should be in your possession with a $25,000 limit.

❖ The balance on your American Express card must be paid in full at the end of each month, unless purchase or charge is more than $75,000. If charge is over $75,000 you may ask American Express for what's called deferred payments,

which is 12 equal payments over a year..
The smart way of going about things
would be to wait until you get the
American Express card limit over
$75,000-$100,000, which I will be
showing you how when we get that
accomplish you can use the funds to start
your business or invest in property.

Step 18: your Visa credit card balance
should be at $10,000, MasterCard balance at
$5000, and Discover card balance at $5000
also. Use your Visa credit card to pay off the
$5000 loan on the Discover card, and call
customer service to increase the limit on the
Discover card to $25,000.

Step 19: use the Discover card to pay off the
MasterCard $5000 loan, then call customer
service saying Triesta limit on the
MasterCard to $25,000.

Step 20: use your Discover card to pay off
the Visa card $5000That as well and called
to increase the visa card to $25,000.

❖ hopefully by now you have a smile on
your face since I just made you $90,000
richer.
❖ Visa card: $25,000
❖ MasterCard: $25,000

- American Express card: $25,000
- Discover card: $15,000
- Bank A Checking's account: $11,000 minus loan payments.
- Bank B savings account: outstanding and in positive status.
- Bank C savings account: outstanding and in positive status.

Step 21: Get A cash advance loan from your Visa card for the whole $25,000 limit and deposit the $25,000 into your TD bank account bank a checking account, bring in your account balance from $11,000-$36,000, In overdraft protection to $50,000-$55,000.

Step 22: no call American Express customer service, and increase the limit of your American Express card from $25,000-$50,000.

Step 23: lastly get a cash advance loan from your MasterCard for the whole $25,000 limit and deposit the $25,000 into the bank a checking account, bringing your account balance from $38,000-$61,000 and the overdraft protection to $80,000-$100,000 then call American express and increase the card limit to $100,000.

Bank A checking account balance: $61,000

Bank B savings account: $500 outstanding and in positive status.

Bank C savings account: $500 outstanding and in positive status.

Commercial cards: both commercial cards of your choosing should have a nice limit if you've been using them and paying it back on time, let's say both have a positive balance of $5000 each.

Utility card: has gas card $500

Visa card: $25,000

MasterCard: $25,000

Discover card: $15,000

Total monetary access: $186,500

If you do not have the $1000 needed to start this process, the easiest way to go about building your credit would be to apply for Kikoff, credit strong, and 2 secured credit cards. Kikoff and credit strong is basically companies that help you boost your credit score by showing up as active account in active loans on your account if you make on-time monthly payments every month. The monthly payment for Kikoff is $20 and the monthly payment for credit strong depending on the plan you chose will vary. The secure credit card is basically like the savings account you're basically only allowed to use the amount of money that you're putting in.

Using tradelines:

A tradeline is a record of any type of credit you have that appears on your credit report. Credit reporting agencies use this term to describe your credit accounts and the information associated with them, including who the lender is and the amount of debt. Each credit account has its own separate tradeline.

Creditors can use data from your tradelines to establish the bigger picture of your likelihood to pay back loans, or whether you seem like a reliable borrower. The data in tradelines is also used to help calculate your credit score.

A tradeline is a record of activity for any one of your credit accounts. Tradelines show up on your credit report as a line that records the trade between you and your creditor. This credit activity gets compiled into your credit report by the major credit reporting agencies. A tradeline is meant to both identify the credit activity or debt and include information about the account.

Tradelines include both installment tradelines, like auto loans, personal loans and student loans, and revolving tradelines, like credit card accounts and other lines of credit.

Looking through the tradelines on your credit report can help you get a better sense of your personal finances. Not only does it make you aware of the information in your credit file, but it also helps you ensure that the information being reported is accurate, so that you aren't harmed by incorrect negative information.

A tradeline isn't just for a lender's benefit — it can provide a wealth of information for you, too. Some details that are generally included in tradelines are:

❖ Reporter information
❖ Account number

- ❖ Equal Credit Opportunity Act (ECOA) codes (such as, A for authorized user, I for individual account, and so on)
- ❖ Type of account
- ❖ Loan amount or credit limit
- ❖ Outstanding balance
- ❖ Payment status
- ❖ Account open and close dates
- ❖ Minimum payment
- ❖ Recent activity on the account
- ❖ Recent balance on credit cards
- ❖ Remarks
- ❖ Delinquency details

Keep in mind that creditors decide what information is included on tradelines, so some of the above might be different or missing from your tradeline, depending on the creditor.

Types of tradelines

Just as you may obtain different types of accounts and credit, credit tradelines come in different types as well. These sections break down some of the most common types of tradelines.

Installment tradelines

An installment tradeline is a fixed loan that you have to pay back. It's essentially when an installment loan of yours, like a student loan, auto loan, mortgage or other personal loan, is included on your credit report. If you take out a $10,000 auto loan, for example, your credit report will show an installment tradeline with the same opening balance.

Revolving tradelines

A revolving tradeline is an open-ended account that creditors and consumers can use multiple times without a fixed timeline. Examples include credit cards or lines of credit, which involve fluctuating account balances within a set credit limit, available credit and monthly payments based on use.

Open account tradelines

An open account tradeline refers to the credit activity record for any currently open credit account you use. This can include the other types of tradelines, but can be more broad, extending to anything defined as an obligation that must be paid in full every month. For example, rental tradelines from third-party rent reporting services, like Level Credit, fall into this category.

How tradelines can affect your credit score

All of your reported credit activity can affect your credit score. Positive information on your credit report helps you achieve good credit; negative information, on the other hand, can hurt your creditworthiness.

Tradelines are part of what makes the information on your credit report. Positive tradelines generally help you build credit, while negative tradelines can lower your credit score. Tradeline information is factored into credit scoring models like FICO® [4] based on the following factors:

❖ **Payment history (35%)**: A consistent on-time payment history helps establish that you're a reliable borrower. Missing or late payments hurt your creditworthiness.
❖ **Amounts owed (30%)**: Having large amounts of debt in relation to your credit limits on your credit report may make

you seem like a riskier borrower, especially if any of your credit accounts are reported as delinquent or sent to collections.

- ❖ **Length of credit history (15%):** The longer your credit history, the more time you have to establish a consistent payment history. Maintaining tradelines in good standing over the course of months or years demonstrates that lenders can trust in you.
- ❖ **Credit mix (10%):** A mix of installment tradelines and revolving tradelines in good standing shows potential lenders that you can handle multiple responsibilities and manage different types of credit well.
- ❖ **New credit (10%):** While hard inquiries to open new tradelines can temporarily lower your credit score a bit, opening accounts is important for your credit mix and, ultimately, establishing the length of your credit history.

Accounts in good standing may have a positive impact.Accounts in good standing are what make up the positive information on your credit report. They're accounts that you manage well through consistent, on-time payments over the length of your credit history.

Generally, maintaining these accounts has a positive impact on your credit score.

For fixed accounts like installment loans, paying the amount of your monthly payment each month helps keep you in good standing. For revolving accounts, paying off your account balance, staying within your credit limit and keeping your credit utilization ratio (your balance on revolving credit divided by your credit limit) low are key strategies.

Some examples of accounts in good standing may include:

❖ Student loans you make regular payments on
❖ Credit cards that you pay the balance in full monthly
❖ A mortgage you've paid consistently for 10 years

If you're struggling with your credit score or to open new tradelines, you may want to consider becoming an authorized user. An authorized user is someone who has permission to use another account holder's credit card to make purchases but is not legally required to pay the debt.

If the credit card company reports the authorized user's account to the three major credit bureaus (Experian, Equifax, and Transunion) it could impact their credit score positively or negatively.

Authorized users should look for a trusted cardholder with a record of on-time payments on their card, a low credit utilization rate (CUR, the total balance divided by the credit limit) and a long account history.

Accounts in bad standing may have a negative impact. Accounts in bad standing make up the negative information on your credit report, and generally hurt your credit score. These are credit accounts that are unpaid, especially to the extent of being considered delinquency or going to collections, that have late or missing payments, high amounts of outstanding debt or high credit utilization ratios.

Some examples of accounts in bad standing may include:

❖ Credit card debt in collections
❖ Accounts (loans or credit) with late payments
❖ Accounts closed due to delinquency

Recent changes in the major credit reporting agencies and major credit scoring models may be more forgiving about some negative information. For example, FICO® 9 scores no longer factor in third-party collection accounts that have been paid off in full, and unpaid medical debt is given less negative weight. However, FICO® 9 isn't as widely used as FICO® 8.

How long do tradelines stay on your credit report?

Typically, a tradeline appears on your credit report when you open a new account. This may have a slight negative impact on your credit score due to a hard inquiry.

Once they're on your credit report:

❖ Tradelines stay on your credit reports as long as accounts are active.
❖ Closed accounts in good standing remain on your report for up to 10 years.
❖ Tradelines with negative history that are closed remain on credit reports for seven years.

Just as tradelines themselves can be positive or negative, whether or not they stay on your credit report can have a positive or negative impact too.

What happens if a tradeline is removed from your credit report?

Tradelines can be removed from your credit report, though the time it takes for them to be removed and the impact that it has on your credit score varies depending on the specific account.

For example, if you decide to stop being an authorized user on another person's credit card, the tradeline might fall off of your credit report in as soon as two months.[1] Closing an account of your own, for positive or negative reasons, generally takes 7 to 10 years.

The positive or negative impact of a tradeline's removal from your credit report depends on the information associated with the account. For example, an account in bad standing that falls off after seven years might cause your score to increase because the negative information associated with it is gone as well.

If there's a negative tradeline on your credit report due to fraud or identity theft, you can have it removed. Be sure to dispute it immediately — the longer fraudulent activity goes unchecked, the more time it takes to repair the impact.

Buying tradelines opens you to unnecessary risk

Buying a tradeline is sometimes presented as a credit repair strategy. It involves paying a third-party service to add you to another person's tradeline, so that their tradeline information appears on your credit report, represented as your own. These are short-term agreements, so you're removed from the tradeline after a designated amount of time.[9]

It might seem similar to becoming an authorized user on someone's account, but there are two key differences:[9]

❖ You don't know the person whose account you're being added to. When you become an authorized user, it's usually on a line of credit held by a friend or family member, not a stranger.
❖ You're paying to be added to the account. Becoming an authorized user, on the other hand, is free.

While it's technically not illegal, buying a tradeline isn't exactly ethical either. Many creditors consider it to be misrepresentative, and the practice poses some risks for borrowers, like identity theft. FICO® 8 has made efforts to lessen the impact that bought tradelines have on someone's credit score, making it even more unclear how helpful a strategy this would be.

Chapter 5:

Business Credit

Depending on your credit and banking history the bank may not be so generous, with allowing you to raise your credit limit so high each month. Don't panic there's always another corner at the end of the block, if this plan is not we're gonna see you liking here's another way you can go about things. It mirrors the previous plan that I explained with the A1 credit plan and using Kikoff and credit strong, Only this time around we're gonna be using the business credit but to get certain loans through your business you have to have a good personal credit too and I already gave you the secret sauce for all of that.

On the first day of the month you need to have $1600 in your possession, just like before we're going to use that cash to open upAccounts with banks of your choosing.

Bank one:

– Open a checking account with the deposit of $100 and try to get interest-bearing chicks.

– Open a savings account with a deposit of $1500, received your save his books and wait three days for this bank to validate and bring this account online.

-on the fourth day, borrow $1400 on a signature loan he was in the savings account as collateral. Terms: 365 day alone with no Pre-payment penalties. A lot of bank to freeze your savings account your first payment will not be due until the 30th day of the following month.

– Use that $1400 to open up another bank account the same day, at a different bank.

• Time elapsed: 4 days

Bank 2:

-Open a savings account and deposit the $1400, just like before received your save in books and wait three days for his bank to validate and bring this account online.

– On the eighth day, borrow $1400 on a signature loan using your savings account as collateral. Terms: 365 day long with no pre-payment penalties. Alarm to freeze your savings account.

– Take your $1400 in cash in on the same day go to another bank.

❖ Time elapsed: 8 Days

Bank 3:

-Open the savings account and deposited $1400 and receive your savings book and wait three days for his bank to validate and bring this account online.

Open – on the 12th day, borrow $1400 on a signature loan using your savings account as collateral. Terms: 365 day long with no prepayment penalties. Allow them to freeze your savings account.

-Take You're $1400 in cash and two days later, begin repayment following the strategy as listed below in the pre-payment schedule.

❖ Time elapsed: 14 Days

Repayment of the signature loans

Bank 1:

-in the first month of the loan, instead of merely making your monthly payment on time, make individual payments on the 14th, the 21st, and the 28th of the month. This will trigger the bank to report to the credit bureau that timely payments are being made on this account.

Note: you are paying a full month ahead of schedule as your payments would not be due until the 30th day of the following month. On the first day of the schedule first month of re-payment, repay the loan entirely. This releases the hold on a saving account at bank one, does freeing the $1500 that you had originally placed there. With it, begin repayment strategy of the loans at bank too.

Bank 2:

-on the seventh day of the scheduled first month of repayment, make payment.

Note: payment was not due until the 30th day of the first month,

– on the 14th day of the schedule first month of your payment, make payment.

– On the 21st day of the schedule first month of repayment, make payment.

– On The 28th day of the schedule first month of repayment, pay off a loan entirely. This obligates bank too to report timely payments to the credit bureau and freeing up the $1400 that you had in your savings account there with it begin repayment strategy of loan and bank 3.

❖ Time elapsed: 60 Days

Bank 3:

-on the 29th day of the schedule first month of repayment, make the first monthly payment.

Note: payment was not due until the 30th day of the second month.

– On the seventh day of the scheduled second month of re-payment, make payment.

– On the 14th day of the scheduled second month of repayment, make payment.

– On the 21st day of the scheduled second month of repayment,Make payment.

– On the first day of the scheduled third month of repayment, pay the loan off entirely. This obligations bank three to report Timely payments to the credit bureau and free the $1400 that you had in your savings account at the bank three. You've paid minimal interest and now I have on record and your credit file, the strongest and best type of credit entries that you can have an America: bank loan credit. If you have followed these instructions, the following table reflects the action that she should have taken.

❖ Time elapsed: 91 Days

Chapter 6:

Business Insurance Policy & Employees

Purchasing a business insurance policy for your new assets is a very imperative step. If you rent office space secure a business property insurance policy. Even if you work from home you will need a separate policy for your business assets. You'll also need liability insurance to protect you from lawsuits should any of your products or services result and someone being injured all property being damaged. Your vendors will typically require a copy of your liability policy to be included within our Pp – request for proposal form. Some vendors even required that they be listed As additionally insured on your policy.

Employees: If your business requires hiring employees, you will also need Workmen's Compensation insurance. This will protect you and your employees should anyone get injured on the job. The cost of this insurance is high, but it varies on the type of workers you have and the level of risk involved in their job function.

Full-time employee: a full-time employee generally works 40 hours a week and has paid overtime for hours work over 40. You must pay Social Security, disability, federal and state Taxes for each employee you hire. However, you have the option as well that you provide health, vacation, or retirement benefits. In many cases, the benefits you provide with the pen on the labor pool you're hired from especially if the skill set required of an employee is scars, be prepared to offer competitive salary and benefit packages to attract the best talent.

Part-time employee: A part-time employee generally works from 15 to 30 hours per week and can be A solid asset and covering ours such as nights and weekends, when your business might need to provide customer service support during off hours. You do not have to pay either medical or retirement benefits to part-time employees.

Contractors: These workers, known as freelancers or 1099 employees, can be very valuable and meeting your business needs; Especially short term, complex jobs without having to add them to your business payroll. Contractors work for hourly rates and are responsible for their own payroll taxes. If you pay a contractor over $600 you are required to send a 1099 tax form to them and the IRS to report their income.

Chapter 7:

Payroll

There are a lot of factors to consider when choosing a payroll service company. The main fact there are easy communication and responsiveness. Responsiveness if there are mistakes with payroll, how quickly can can it be corrected and paychecks be re-issued? Easy communication – how hard is it for the company to add new employees to your system? Update in the payroll this should be quick and easy.

Payroll services works in harmony with your business account to pay all employees and yourself the employer. Basic monthly payroll services include paycheck processing, online account access, quarterly tax filings, and direct deposits. Prices can range from $20-$150 per month, depending on the frequency of payroll and the number of employees. Per check fee if applicable range from $.75 to two dollars or more, and additional fees for adding new employees, check delivery, and extra reporting are typical. Get a full breakdown of all fees before committing to the provider.

Lastly make sure you have W-2 and W9 forms updated annually, and all full-time and 1099 contract employees. Your accountant can handle the Basic payroll taxes FICA, state taxes, Social Security deductions, disability contributions, and others. When ordering your checks from the payroll service you choose, make sure your business name, address, telephone number, and website are listed on each check. You can also make an issue your own business/payroll checks but using Business check softwares. One business check software I would recommend would be Versa Check you can order the software through their website onversacheck.com or you can order it from amazon.com or go to any office supply store and buy it in person.

Chapter 8:

Tax Write-Offs

A tax deduction (or "tax write-off") is an expense that you can deduct from your taxable income. You take the amount of the expense and subtract that from your taxable income. Essentially, tax write-offs allow you to pay a smaller tax bill. But the expense has to fit the IRS criteria of a tax deduction.

Below you'll find a comprehensive list of write-offs commonly available to self employed businesses that are organized as sole proprietorship or partnerships. Some of these are directly related to running a business, and some are more personal deductions that a small business owner should be aware of.

Making the most of all your available tax deductions can save you hundreds—even thousands—of dollars at tax time.

Let's look at an example.

I am a self-employed publisher and had $60,000 in self employment income in 2022. I had to pay 15.3% self employment (SE) tax plus income tax based on my individual tax rate. The SE tax on $60,000 is

$8,478 (generally only 92.35% of SE income is subject to SE tax) and the income tax is $4,865, for a total of $13,343.

(For simplicity, I am single with no children and no other types of taxable income to consider.)

In early 2023, I hired an accountant that located $6,000 worth of contractor expenses that I was not aware of. These expenses count as tax deductions and reduce my net self employment income to $54,000.

Now, with $54,000 in taxable self employment income, i has to pay $7,630 in SE tax and $4,200 in income tax, for a total of $11,830.

Adding the additional business expenses saved me over $1,500 in taxes!

By locating the $6,000 in contractor expenses, The account was able to reduce my tax liability by over $1,500 dollars. A nice saving he can use to upgrade his laptop this year.

Repeat this for all the available deductions I had expenses for, and I can significantly reduce the income I have to pay taxes on—saving me thousands of dollars.

Staying on top of your deductions

As a small business owner, it can be difficult to know what deductions are relevant to you.

Many people struggle to stay on top of their deductions year round and instead try to piece things together at year end and run into difficulties. Remember that restaurant expense you incurred in January last year? Most people don't, and therefore they miss this tax write off. Add them all up and you're missing out on a lot of tax savings.

That's where bookkeeping comes in.

To claim these deductions, you'll need to keep accurate records and stay on top of your monthly bookkeeping.

Ongoing bookkeeping is critical to help you tally up your deductions. If you don't have a good DIY setup you're happy with, Look up some businesses that offers book keeping.

Bank fees

Having separate bank accounts and credit cards for your business is always a good idea. If your bank or credit card company charges annual or monthly service charges, transfer fees, or overdraft fees, these are deductible. You can also deduct merchant or transaction fees paid to a third-party payment processor, such as PayPal or Stripe.

You cannot deduct fees related to your personal bank accounts or credit cards.

Business meals

You can generally deduct 50% of qualifying food and beverage costs. To be eligible for the deduction:

❖ The expense must be an ordinary and necessary part of carrying on your business

❖ The meal cannot be lavish or extravagant under the circumstances

❖ The business owner or an employee must be present at the meal

You can deduct 100% of the cost of providing meals to employees, such as buying pizza for dinner when your team is working late. Meals provided at office parties and picnics are also 100% deductible.

Be sure to keep documentation for the outing that includes the amount of each expense, the date and place of the meal, and the business relationship of the person you dined with.

A good way to do this is to record the purpose of the meal and what you discussed on the back of the receipt.

Business insurance

You can deduct the premiums you pay for business insurance.

This may include:

* Property coverage for your furniture, equipment, and buildings
* Liability coverage
* Group health, dental and vision insurance for employees
* Professional liability or malpractice insurance
* Workers compensation coverage
* Auto insurance for business vehicles
* Life insurance that covers employees, as long as the business or business owner is not a beneficiary on the policy
* Business interruption insurance that covers lost profits if your business is shut down due to fire or another cause

Business use of your car

Do you use your vehicle for business? If you use your vehicle solely for business purposes, then you can deduct the entire cost of operating the vehicle. If you use it for both business and personal trips, you can only deduct the costs associated with business-related usage.

There are two methods for deducting vehicle expenses, and you can choose whichever one gives you a greater tax benefit.

❖ Standard mileage rate. Multiply the miles driven for business during the year by a standard mileage rate. For miles driven in 2022, it is $0.585 per mile from January 1 to June 30 and $0.625 per mile from July 1 to December 31. In 2023, the mileage rate is increased to $0.655 per mile.

❖ Actual expense method. Track all of the costs of operating the vehicle for the year, including gas, oil, repairs, tires, insurance, registration fees, and lease payments. Multiply those expenses by the percentage of miles driven for business. Note that you cannot switch from the actual expense method to the standard mileage method on the same vehicle.

Both methods require that you track your business miles for the year. You can keep a detailed log of your business miles, use an app to track your trips, or reconstruct a mileage log using other documents, such as calendars or appointment books. If you keep a mileage log, clearly document the miles driven, time and place, and business purpose of your trip.

Note that you cannot count the miles driven while commuting between your home and your regular place of business. These costs are considered personal commuting expenses.

Contract Labour

If you hire freelancers or independent contractors to help in your business, you can deduct their fees as a business expense.

Just remember, if you pay a contractor $600 or more during the tax year, you're required to send them a **Form 1099-NEC** by January 31st of the following year.

Depreciation

When you purchase furniture, equipment, and other business assets, depreciation rules require you to spread the costs of those assets over the years you'll use them rather than deducting the full cost in a single hit.

Expanding these items upfront is more attractive because of the quicker tax benefit. Fortunately, the IRS gives business owners several ways to write off the full cost in one year.

❖ De minimis safe harbor election. Small businesses can elect to expense assets that cost less than $2,500 per item in the year they are purchased.

❖ Section 179 deduction. The **Section 179 deduction** allows business owners to deduct up to $1,080,000 of property placed in service during the tax year. This includes new and used business property and "off-the-shelf" software. The Section 179 deduction is limited to the business's taxable income, so claiming it cannot create a net loss on your return. However, any unused Section 179 deduction can be carried forward and deducted on next year's return.

❖ Bonus depreciation. Businesses can take advantage of **bonus depreciation** to deduct 100% of the cost of machinery, equipment, computers, appliances, and furniture.

If you purchased a new vehicle during the tax year, the IRS limits write-offs for passenger vehicles. In the first year, if you don't claim bonus depreciation, the maximum depreciation deduction is $10,100. If you do claim bonus depreciation, the maximum write off is $18,100.

Depreciation is more complicated than your average deduction, so i recommend reading more on it and asking your accountant which assets you can deduct in your business.

Education

Education costs are fully deductible when they add value to your business and increase your expertise. In order to decide if your class or workshop qualifies, the IRS will look at whether the expense maintains or improves skills that are required in your current business.

The following list contains examples of valid business education expenses:

❖ Classes to improve skills in your field

❖ Seminars and webinars

- ❖ Subscriptions to trade or professional publications
- ❖ Books tailored to your industry
- ❖ Workshops to increase your expertise and skills
- ❖ Transportation expenses to and from classes

Keep in mind that any education costs that would qualify you for a new career, or costs related to education outside of the realm of your business, don't qualify as business tax deductions.

Home office expenses

If you use a home office for your business, you may be able to deduct a portion of your housing expenses against business income. There are two ways to deduct home office expenses.

- ❖ Simplified method. You can deduct $5 per square foot of your home that is used for business, up to a maximum of 300 square feet.

- ❖ Standard method. Track all actual expenses of maintaining your home, such as mortgage interest or rent, utilities, real estate taxes, housekeeping and landscaping service, homeowners association fees, and repairs.

❖ Multiply these expenses by the percentage of your home devoted to business use.

To qualify for the home office deduction, you need to measure up in two areas:

❖ Regular and exclusive use. To pass the regular and exclusive use requirement, you must regularly use your home office exclusively for conducting business activities. A desk that doubles as your kitchen table won't work. You don't need to dedicate an entire room to your business, but your work area should have clearly identifiable boundaries. You may want to keep photos of your home office workspace with your tax documentation as evidence in case the IRS selects your return for audit.

❖ Principal place of business. Your home office must be your principal place of business. This means you spend the most time and conduct important business activities here.

If you use the standard method for calculating your home office deduction, you'll need to file **Form 8829** along with your Schedule C.

Interest

If you take out a loan or use a credit card to cover business expenses, you can deduct the interest paid to your lender or credit card company as long as you meet the following requirements:

❖ You are legally liable for the debt. For example, if your parents take out a second mortgage on their home to help you start a business, you are not legally liable for the debt. In that case, interest on the loan is not deductible, even if you make all of the payments on the mortgage.

❖ Both you and the lender intend for the debt to be repaid. A loan that doesn't have to be repaid is a gift.

❖ You and the lender have a true debtor/creditor relationship. The IRS tends to scrutinize loans between related parties, such as family members. If you use the accrual method of accounting, you cannot deduct interest owed to a related person until the payment is made.

Keep in mind that if a loan is part business and part personal, you need to divide the interest between the business and personal parts of the loan.

Legal and professional fees

Legal and professional fees that are necessary and directly related to running your business are deductible. These include fees charged by lawyers, accountants, bookkeepers, tax preparers, and online bookkeeping services.

If the fees include payments for work of a personal nature (for example, making a will), you can only deduct the part of the fee that's related to the business.

Moving expenses

The Tax Cuts and Jobs Act of 2017 eliminated the deduction for moving expenses for all nonmilitary individuals, but businesses can still deduct the cost of moving business equipment, supplies and inventory from one business location to another.

Be sure to keep good records to substantiate all costs associated with your business move.

Rent expense

If you rent a business location or equipment for your business, you can deduct the rental payments as a business expense.

Keep in mind, rent paid on your home should not be deducted as a business expense, even if you have a home office. That rent can be deducted as a part of home office expenses.

Salaries and benefits

Salaries, benefits and even vacation time paid to employees are generally tax-deductible, as long as they meet a few criteria:

- ❖ The "employee" is not the sole proprietor, a partner, or an LLC member
- ❖ The salary is reasonable, ordinary, and necessary
- ❖ The services were actually provided

Taxes and licenses

You can deduct various taxes and licenses related to your business. This may include:

- ❖ State income taxes
- ❖ Payroll taxes

- Personal property taxes
- Real estate taxes paid on business property
- Sales tax
- Excise taxes
- Fuel taxes
- Business licenses

Telephone and internet expenses

If telephone and internet services are integral to your business, they can be deductible business expenses.

Keep in mind, if you use a landline at home, you cannot deduct the cost of your first line, even if you use it solely for work. However, if you have a second landline devoted to the business, the cost of that line is deductible.

If you use your cell phone and internet connection for both personal and business reasons, you can only deduct the percentage allocated to business use. Keep an itemized bill or other detailed records to prove the amount of business use in case your return is audited.

Travel expenses

For a trip to qualify as business travel, it has to be ordinary, necessary, and away from your tax home. Your tax home is the entire city or area in which you conduct business, regardless of where you live. You need to travel away from your tax home for longer than a normal day's work, requiring you to sleep or rest en route.

Deductible, IRS approved business travel expenses include:

- ❖ Travel to and from your destination by plane, train, bus, or car
- ❖ Using your car while at a business location
- ❖ Parking and toll fees
- ❖ The cost of taxis and other methods of transportation used on a business trip
- ❖ Meals and lodging
- ❖ Tips
- ❖ Laundry and dry cleaning while on a business trip
- ❖ Business calls
- ❖ Shipping of baggage and sample or display materials to your destination

❖ Other similar ordinary and necessary expenses related to your business travel

Remember to keep records that include the amount of each expense, as well as dates of return/departure, details of the trip (whom you met with), a mileage log if you drove your own vehicle, and the business reason for the trip.

Personal tax deductions for business owners

The above-mentioned deductions can be claimed on **Schedule C or Form 1065's Schedule K-1**, but there are a few other tax breaks small business owners commonly claim on their individual returns.

Charitable contributions

Sole proprietorship, LLCs, and partnerships cannot deduct charitable contributions as a business expense, but the business owner may be able to claim the deduction on their personal tax return.

To qualify, the donation must be made to a **qualified organization.**

Starting with 2020 returns, taxpayers can claim up to $300 of cash contributions as an "above-the-line" deduction on Form 1040. To deduct more than that, the business owner has to itemize deductions on Schedule A attached to Form 1040.

Child and dependent care expenses

If you pay someone to care for a child or another dependent while you work, you may be able to claim the Child and Dependent Care Credit. To qualify, the person receiving the card must be a child (under age 13) or a spouse or other dependent who is physically or mentally incapable of self-care.

The credit is worth between 20% and 35% of your allowable expenses, depending on your income. Allowable expenses are limited to $4,000 for the care of one dependent and $8,000 if you paid for the care of two or more dependents. IRS Publication 503 provides more information on the Child and Dependent Care Credit. You'll need to attach Form 2441 to your Form 1040 to claim the credit.

Retirement contributions

You can deduct contributions to employee retirement accounts as a business expense. The amount you can deduct depends on the type of plan you have. Check out the IRS's tips for calculating your own retirement plan contribution and deduction for more information.

Health care expenses

In addition to insurance premiums, you can deduct other out-of-pocket medical costs, such as office co-pays and the cost of prescriptions. These costs are normally included on itemized deductions on Schedule A.

Self-employed business owners can also deduct health insurance premiums for themselves, their spouse, and dependents on Schedule 1 attached to their Form 1040. However, if you are eligible to participate in a plan through your spouse's employer, then the business can't deduct those premiums.

The bottom line

Tax deductions are an essential way to minimize the amount of tax you have to pay, and good record keeping will ensure you get to keep those deductions if the IRS ever comes knocking.

Have your team of dedicated bookkeepers at Bench track all of the expenses related to running your business to ensure you're taking advantage of every legitimate deduction. Send Bench's books to your accountant at year end, or let us take the tax filing off your plate for good!

Chapter 9:

Buy Real Estate With No Money

Letters of credit are often used in real estate transactions to secure obligations. Instead of providing a cash deposit, a buyer, borrower or tenant may secure its obligations under a contract of sale, loan commitment, or lease with a letter of credit. An attorney representing a party giving or receiving a letter of credit needs to understand the law of letters of credit, their risks and benefits. Because real estate attorneys often lack that expertise, this article is intended to provide a short primer on letters of credit for real estate attorneys.

WHAT IS A LETTER OF CREDIT?

A letter of credit is a commitment made by a bank or other party (the "issuer"), upon the application of the issuer's client (the "applicant"), to pay the amount of the letter of credit to a third party (the "beneficiary") upon the beneficiary's submission to the issuer of the documents listed in the letter of credit. By separate reimbursement agreement, the applicant agrees to reimburse the issuer for any liability incurred by the issuer under the letter of credit. Although letters of credit may theoretically be issued by anyone, bank letters of credit are typically used in commerce. For example, a tenant may request its bank to issue a letter of credit to the landlord as security. In such a transaction, the tenant is the applicant, the bank is the issuer and the landlord is the beneficiary.

WHAT DOES A LETTER OF CREDIT LOOK LIKE?

Letters of credit are typically one or two-page documents. Attached to these materials is a form of letter of credit. Each bank, however, issues its own form of letter of credit and may refuse to use a form dictated by the beneficiary. Accordingly, the beneficiary's attorney should be prepared to review the bank's form to determine if it is appropriate.

WHAT ARE THE ADVANTAGES AND DISADVANTAGES OF LETTERS OF CREDIT?

General

Letters of credit are generally regarded as superior to cash security in a bankruptcy. However, because letters of credit involve some disadvantages (which may be ignored in the rush for a more secure form of security), it is important for the landlord/seller/lender to make an informed decision about whether or not to require the tenant/buyer/borrower to secure its obligations with a letter of credit. This article will focus on the use of letters of credit in lease transactions, but many of the principles set out below apply to other transactions.

Bankruptcy Considerations

Because letters of credit are viewed as more advantageous in bankruptcy than cash security, security in the form of a letter of credit may be required by landlords leasing space to high risk tenants (such as start up companies, restaurant tenants, and dot coma), sellers contracting to sell land to a shell company, and/or banks making loans to shell companies.

Bankruptcy basically provides a means for rehabilitating bankrupt debtors (through Chapter 11 proceedings) and/or distributing the bankrupt's debtor's assets to its creditors. Secured creditors are, in theory, entitled to the benefit of their security notwithstanding the debtor's bankruptcy.

Unsecured creditors usually receive a fraction of what's owed them because they are part of a large pool of creditors paid out of assets that are not encumbered by security interests.

The landlord's right to cash security is generally secure in a tenant bankruptcy, notwithstanding the fact that courts have generally rejected (or failed to respond to) arguments that a landlord has a perfected security interest in cash security.

The Bankruptcy Code (11 U.S.C. §1 et seq.) allows creditors to exercise offset rights against bankrupt debtors as long as such offset rights are available under state or federal law and the applicable conditions are met. 11 U.S.C. §553. Accordingly, if a creditor owes a bankrupt debtor money, it may offset against that obligation amounts due from the debtor to the creditor.

Offset rights, as applied in leasing transactions, allow the landlord to offset amounts owed by the bankrupt tenant to the landlord (i.e., rent arrears) against amounts owed by the landlord to the tenant (i.e., the tenant's cash security deposit). Courts have held that a landlord may exercise such offset rights with respect to a bankrupt tenant's security deposit. E.g., In Re Communicable Central, Inc., 106 B.R. 540 (Bankr. N.D. Ill. 1989).

However, the landlord cannot exercise its offset rights against cash security immediately. When a debtor is placed in bankruptcy, all actions and proceedings against the bankrupt's estate are automatically stayed. See 11 U.S.C. §362. Section 362 has been broadly construed to stay many different kinds of actions against the debtor, including any attempt by a landlord to draw on a bankrupt tenant's security deposit.

Because a cash security deposit is property of the tenant-debtor (i.e., part of the bankrupt's estate), the automatic stay prevents the landlord from drawing on any unapplied security deposit until the end of the bankruptcy case (unless the landlord can persuade the court to lift the automatic stay as to the security deposit).

At the end of the bankruptcy case, the landlord will be able to exercise its offset rights and apply the security deposit to any rent arrears. However, it may take years for the bankruptcy case to end.

Because a letter of credit evidences the obligation of the issuing bank to the landlord beneficiary, not the obligation of the tenant to the landlord, the letter of credit and its proceeds are not viewed as part of the tenant-debtor's estate and therefore are not subject to the automatic stay.

Accordingly, if a tenant in default files for bankruptcy, the automatic stay does not bar the landlord from drawing on the letter of credit. In Re Farm Fresh Supermarkets of Maryland, Inc., 257 B.R. 770 (Bankr. Md. 2001) (landlord did not violate automatic stay by drawing down letter of credit after tenant's bankruptcy filing and was not required to turn over letter of credit proceeds to bankrupt tenant's estate, the court reasoning that the letter of credit proceeds were not property of the bankrupt's estate); see also In Re Elegant Merchandising, Inc., 41 B.R. 398 (Bankr. S.D.N.Y. 1984) (letter of credit and its proceeds are not the property of the bankrupt=s estate; therefore, the draw down of a letter of credit does not violate automatic stay).

Another possible bankruptcy advantage in lease transactions to a letter of credit – but one rejected by recent cases – is the possibility of avoiding the bankruptcy cap on the landlord's damages. If a bankrupt tenant rejects a lease, the landlord's claim for damages is capped by Sec. 502(b) (6) of the Bankruptcy Code.

Under that Section, the landlord's "allowable" claim is limited to the sum of (1) the rent due as of the filing of the bankruptcy petition (or the date of lease termination if termination occurs earlier), and (2) the greater of (A) one year's rent (calculated without any reference to acceleration of rents), and (B) 15% of the rent due for the remaining term of the lease (not to exceed three years' rent).

Bankruptcy courts have held that resetting proceeds (which are received from a third party) are applied against the landlord's gross damages and the reduced amount capped. Cash security deposits, on the other hand, are applied against the landlord's capped damages claim, rather than against the landlord's gross lease termination damages, thus eliminating the landlord's ability to take cash in hand and apply it against all its damages (at least, to the extent those damages exceed the cap), and also reducing the landlord's potential claim against the bankrupt estate.

See Oldden v. Tonto Realty Corp., 143 F.2d 916, 962-63 (2d Cir. 1944); In re Communicable Central, Inc., 106 B.R. 540, 1989 Bankr. LEXIS 1882 (Bankr. N.D. Ill. 1989); Lake Parkway Associates v. Noble, 2004 WL 784413 (N.Y. City Ct.); and legislative history found at H.R. Rep. No. 95-595, 95th Cong., 1st Sess. 353-354 (1977); S. Rep. No. 95-989, 95th Cong., 2nd Sess. 63-64 (1978).

Because the proceeds of a letter of credit (like reletting proceeds) are paid by a third party, landlords have argued that the proceeds of a letter of credit should be applied against the landlord's gross damages rather than its capped claim. Recent cases, however, have rejected this argument. See In re Mayan Networks Corporation, 2004 Bankr. Lexis 184 (9th Cir. 2004); and In re PPI Enterprises, Inc., 324 F.3d 197 (3rd Cir. 2003).

The Mayan and PPI courts held that if a letter of credit serves as a lease security deposit, existing case law that requires the application of cash security deposits to the landlord's capped claim, also requires application of the letter of credit proceeds to the landlord's capped claim.

The concurring opinion in Mayan, however, suggested that the proceeds of a letter of credit should be applied against the landlord's gross damages (rather than its capped claim) if the bankrupt's estate is not liable for more than the capped claim.

Accordingly, if (a) the reimbursement agreement with the bank is secured by a third party personal guaranty, rather than the debtor's assets, or (b) the lease is guaranteed by a principal of the tenant (presumably capped at an agreed amount) and the guaranty is secured by a letter of credit in turn secured by the guarantor's assets, the letter of credit proceeds should be applied against the landlord's gross damages rather than its capped damages.

However, as the Fifth Circuit has recently pointed out, if the landlord does not file a claim against the tenant in bankruptcy court, the cap on the landlord's damages never comes into play and the landlord should be free to apply the letter of credit against the landlord's gross damages.

In re Stone bridge Technologies, Inc., 430 F.3d 260 (5th Cir. 2005).

In Stone bridge, the landlord drew on the letter of credit after commencement of the tenant's bankruptcy, but filed no claim for damages.

The issuing bank, with the consent of the bankruptcy trustee, then drew on a certificate of deposit it was holding as security for the tenant's reimbursement obligations under the letter of credit.

The trustee then was given an assignment of the issuing bank's alleged claims against the landlord for improper draw and negligent misrepresentation (there was an issue as to whether the landlord breached the lease when it drew on the letter of credit), and then sued the landlord to recover the letter of credit proceeds (a) in its capacity as assignee of the issuing bank, and (b) in its capacity as trustee on the grounds that the total amount of the letter of credit and cash security exceeded the amount the landlord could recover as damages under §502 (b)(6).

The trial court held that the landlord had breached the lease by failing to give the tenant notice of default and opportunity to cure before drawing on the letter of credit, but was overruled on this point.

The Fifth Circuit held that the landlord's motion in bankruptcy court for payment of rent constituted the required "notice," that the landlord's damages were then fixed by the rent acceleration provision of the lease, and that the letter of credit proceeds were correctly drawn down and applied to the accelerated damages.

The trial court also held against the landlord on the §502(b)(6) cap, holding that the security deposit had to be subtracted from the landlord's capped claim, citing the PPI case; and then ordered the landlord to disgorge the excess of the security above the capped claim.

On this point the trial court was also overruled, the Fifth Circuit holding that §502(b)(6) caps the landlord's claim for damages, and that if the landlord made no claim for damages in the bankruptcy court, its damages could not be capped and the landlord was therefore free to use the proceeds of the letter of credit.

There are some lessons to be learned from these cases. First, if the landlord requires the letter of credit to be secured by a third party's assets (e.g., the landlord requires a 3rd party guaranty secured by a letter of credit that is in turn secured by the 3rd party's assets), the landlord can argue that the it should not be subject to the bankruptcy cap since the letter of credit is not secured by the bankrupt tenant's assets.

Second, as was made abundantly clear by the Stone bridge Technologies case, it is a good idea, where possible, to require the tenant to secure its lease obligations with a letter of credit in a sum large enough to ensure that the landlord will feel comfortable if it relies solely on the letter of credit to cover its damages, explicitly negates any notice requirement as a condition to drawing on the letter of credit, and includes an acceleration of rent provision.

Other Considerations -- From the Landlord's Perspective

There are some disadvantages to a letter of credit from the landlord=s standpoint. It is not as readily available as cash in the landlord=s account because the landlord must present the letter of credit to the issuing bank for payment. There is also the risk that (a) a defective presentation of the letter of credit will be made to the bank as the letter of credit is expiring, (b) the landlord=s staff will ignore, misplace, or fail to deal with a critical bank notice (for example, a notice that the bank is not renewing the letter of credit), (c) the landlord will fail to advise the issuer of a change of address and, as a result, a critical bank notice is sent to the wrong address and not received by landlord, and (d) a litigious tenant may seek to enjoin payment of the letter of credit on frivolous grounds and the lower courts, because of their lack of familiarity with the law, may (at least initially) issue the injunction.

On the other hand, because letters of credit can be superior to cash if a tenant files for bankruptcy, start up tenants (who have a high risk of failure) entering into significant leases are usually requested to provide letters of credit in lieu of cash security.

Other Considerations -- From the Tenant's Perspective

For a tenant operating a small business, a letter of credit may not constitute an attractive form of security because the issuing bank may require the tenant to secure repayment of the letter of credit with an equivalent amount of cash and, in addition, the tenant will have to pay an annual fee to the bank. Accordingly, the net result will be that the tenant loses the use of an amount of cash equal to the security and, in addition, pays a fee for the issuance and maintenance of the letter of credit.

A tenant with more capital or with an open line of credit, may be able to obtain a letter of credit without segregating cash collateral to secure its reimbursement obligation to the issuing bank. For such an entity, use of a letter of credit as security will have some appeal, because it will not be required to tie up any cash to secure the letter of credit and it will pay a relatively small fee to the bank for the annual maintenance of the letter of credit.

COMMERCIAL LETTERS OF CREDIT AND STANDBY LETTERS OF CREDIT

There are 2 forms of letter of credit: the standby letter of credit and the commercial letter of credit.

A commercial letter of credit is issued when the parties intend to effect payment of an obligation through a letter of credit. For example, a commodity seller wants assurance that it will be paid before it loads the commodity on a ship to be transported to the buyer's country.

The buyer, on the other hand, does not want to pay before the commodity has been loaded and inspected. To solve the problem, the buyer will have its bank issue a commercial letter of credit to the seller. The letter of credit will be payable to the seller upon the seller's presentation to the issuer of a bill of lading and inspection certificate.

A standby letter of credit is intended to stand as security. It will only be paid if the applicant defaults in performing its obligations to the beneficiary. Standby letters of credit are used in lease transactions as security.

GOVERNING CODES

Letters of credit are subject to Article 5 of the Uniform Commercial Code. However, the Uniform Commercial Code (as amended by the 1995 revisions) expressly provides that the parties to a letter of credit may choose to adopt another rule of practice or code to govern the rights of the parties, except as to those rights that are not variable under the Uniform Commercial Code (including the obligation of good faith).

There are several codes and rules of practice that have been adopted with respect to letters of credit. The most commonly used codes are: (a) The International Standby Practices ISP 98 (AISP@)

published by the International Chamber of Commerce, which was drafted specifically to govern standby letters of credit, and (2) the Uniform Customs and Practice for Documentary Credits Publication 600 of 2007 published by the International Chamber of Commerce (the "UCP"), which was drafted with respect to commercial letters of credit but which is frequently used with respect to standby letters of credit.

Opinions have been issued by the International Chamber of Commerce Banking Commission with respect to letters of credit.

The letter of credit itself will state what practice or convention governs it. Because the ISP was drafted specifically to cover standby letters of credit, landlords should generally request that the letter of credit be governed by the ISP. However, because the ISP is a late comer to the field of letters of credit and banks are more familiar with the UCP, many banks provide that their letters of credit are governed by the UCP. Both codes deal comprehensively and well with the issues raised by letters of credit, and landlord attorneys should be comfortable with both codes.

PRESENTATION, JURISDICTION AND VENUE

If the issuing bank does not have offices in the landlord=s jurisdiction, the landlord will have to travel to the issuing bank's offices to draw on the letter of credit, which may be inconvenient, but is possible. Even if the letter of credit is issued by a local bank, the landlord may have to travel to present the letter of credit for payment because local banks sometimes consolidate their letter of credit operations in other states. For example, as of February 2005, two New York banks (Chase and Citibank) require presentation of letters of credit at their Florida offices for payment.

Under the ISP, the letter of credit should expressly indicate where the letter of credit must be presented for payment. ISP §3.01. If the letter of credit does not so indicate, the presentation must be made at the place of business from which the letter of credit was issued. ISP §3.04.

Accordingly, if the letter of credit does not say where the presentation must be made, but indicates that the letter of credit was issued at the bank's Fort Lauderdale office, presentation must be made at the Fort Lauderdale office.

If the letter of credit must be presented for payment in another jurisdiction, the landlord should be advised of that fact.

Presentation for payment is made when the bank receives the necessary demand and/or documents. ISP §3.02. Accordingly, the letter of credit and any accompanying documents do not need to be presented in person.

They can be mailed. In addition, the letter of credit can be modified to provide for a fax presentation followed by a federal express (or other) delivery of the documents, or other means of presentation.

If the letter of credit must be presented at the bank=s offices in a foreign jurisdiction, and the letter of credit is dishonored, what law will apply? Article 5 of the Uniform Commercial Code provides that the liability of the issuer is governed by the law of the jurisdiction in which it is located. Under UCC '5-116, the issuer is considered to be located at the address indicated in its undertaking.

Accordingly, if the letter of credit indicates that the issuer=s address is in the State of Washington, Washington State law may apply unless the letter of credit otherwise provides. If the leased property is in New York and the landlord wants to be certain that New York law will apply, the letter of credit should be drafted to provide that it will be governed by the law of the State of New York as to matters not covered by the ISP or the UCP.

If the issuer does not have offices in the jurisdiction in which the leased premises are located, a serious issue that can arise is the question of the appropriate venue for any litigation involving the letter of credit. Jurisdiction and venue may be determined by agreement. UCC '5-116(e).

Accordingly, if the issuing bank is a foreign bank with unknown or tenuous contacts with the state in which the leased premises are located, the landlord's attorney should insist that the letter of credit provide that local courts have jurisdiction and that the venue of any litigation be in the state and county in which the leased premises are located.

The resolution of venue issues, of course, does not solve all problems. If the issuing bank has no assets in the jurisdiction in which the premises are located, any judgment will have to be enforced out-of-state, increasing litigation expense.

Foreign banks sometimes propose that the letter of credit be Advised@ through or Confirmed@ by a local bank. An advising bank merely verifies that it has checked the letter of credit=s apparent authenticity in accordance with standard practice and that it has accurately advised the beneficiary of what it has received – in short, an advising bank verifies in a somewhat qualified fashion the authenticity of the letter of credit. ISP §2.05.

A confirming bank, on the other hand, assumes the issuer=s obligation to make payment on the letter of credit. ISP §2.01d. Accordingly, if a tenant proposes to deliver a letter of credit from an out-of-state bank and the landlord is concerned about venue and enforcement issues, the landlord=s attorney should insist that the tenant have (a) a local bank issue the letter of credit (which can be effected through inter-bank arrangements), or (b) a local bank act as a confirming bank, or (c) the issuing bank consent to jurisdiction and venue in the local courts (understanding, however, that the landlord may have to travel to the state in which the out-of-state bank is located to collect on any judgment).

A sample New York provision providing for local jurisdiction and venue is as follows:

Issuer, for itself, its representatives, successors and assigns, agrees that the venue of any action or proceeding with respect to this letter of credit shall be in any court of competent jurisdiction in the County of New York, State of New York; that any such court shall have jurisdiction over such action or proceeding; and that New York law shall govern the construction, interpretation, performance, and/or enforcement of this Letter of Credit, to the extent state law is applicable.

LETTERS OF CREDIT ARE IRREVOCABLE

A letter of credit cannot be revoked by the applicant. The issuing bank is required to pay the letter of credit in accordance with its terms, whether or not the applicant actually authorized the issuance of the letter of credit, whether or not the beneficiary is actually entitled to payment from the applicant, and whether or not the issuer has knowledge of any default under the agreement between the beneficiary and applicant or other underlying transaction.

See ICP §1.06, Because the letter of credit is irrevocable, it cannot be amended or canceled (except in accordance with its terms) without the consent of the beneficiary.

A letter of credit subject to ISP 98 is automatically irrevocable, whether or not the letter of credit expressly provides that it is irrevocable. ISP §1.06(a). The UCP, on the other hand, provides that a letter of credit may be either revocable or irrevocable and that if nothing is said in the letter of credit, the letter of credit is deemed irrevocable. UCP Article 6.

AUTOMATICALLY RENEWING LETTERS OF CREDIT (EVERGREEN)

Because a letter of credit represents an irrevocable obligation of the bank to a third party, it is unusual for banks to issue letters of credit for a term longer than 1 year, although banks will issue somewhat longer letters of credit (e.g., 2 or 3 years) for good customers. The bank does not want to be in the position of having issued a 10-year letter of credit for a customer that may leave it after 3 years.

On the other hand, a lease generally represents a long-term obligation, and no landlord would be willing to accept a letter of credit with a one-year term that had to be replaced annually. To solve this problem the "evergreen" letter of credit was created.

An evergreen letter of credit provides that it will automatically renew for successive periods (typically, 1-year periods) unless the issuing bank gives the beneficiary notice prior to the expiration date that it elects not to renew.

In a typical lease scenario, a 1-year letter of credit is issued to the landlord that provides that it will automatically renew for successive one-year periods unless, at least 60 days prior to the applicable expiration date, the bank notifies the landlord that it is not renewing.

The lease must provide that if the landlord receives such a notice of non-renewal, the landlord may present the letter of credit for payment unless the tenant replaces the letter of credit within an agreed period (e.g., at least 15 days prior to the expiration of the existing letter of credit).

A letter of credit, even if evergreen, must have a final expiration date – a date beyond which the letter of credit will expire with no further renewals.

That date should be after the stated expiration date of the lease, so that the landlord continues to hold security if the tenant holds over or is in default at the end of the term of the lease. The time period is negotiable. Landlords usually negotiate for a 90-day period, in part to avoid possible bankruptcy problems if the tenant files for bankruptcy after the expiration of the lease. Tenants usually negotiate for a 30-day period.

The evergreen feature of a letter of credit works only if the landlord receives notice of non-renewal when the bank sends one. The letter of credit will include a notice address for the beneficiary. If the landlord's address changes, it must ensure that the bank will send the non-renewal notice to the landlord's new address.

If the bank refuses to include in the letter of credit a mechanism for changing the landlord's notice address (which is not uncommon), the landlord must include in the lease a provision that requires the tenant to cooperate in effecting reasonable amendments to the letter of credit and then have the letter of credit amended to reflect the landlord's new address.

Another possible way of dealing with the problem of the changing address is to require in the letter of credit that a copy of any non-renewal notice be sent to the landlord=s attorney. However, the issuing bank may be unwilling to add such a provision.

LETTERS OF CREDIT MAY BE DRAWN IN FULL OR IN PARTIAL DRAWINGS

Under the ISP, partial drawings and multiple presentations are automatically permitted, unless the letter of credit, by its terms, prohibits partial drawings or multiple presentations. ISP §3.08.

CHANGE IN BENEFICIARY: DEATH, INCAPACITY, SUCCESSION

The ISP provides that a successor (as opposed to a transferee) of the beneficiary "may" be treated by the issuing bank as if it was an authorized transferee of the letter of credit if specified documentation is delivered to the bank. ISP §§6.11 -- 6.14.

Accordingly, a bank "may" pay the letter of credit to the executor of a deceased individual beneficiary, or to the successor by merger of a corporate beneficiary, or to the personal representative of an incapacitated beneficiary. Among other things, the bank may require indemnities and an opinion of counsel.

ISP §6.12. Because the bank is not required to recognize a successor, the lease should include a provision requiring the tenant to cooperate in effecting any reasonable amendment of the letter of credit, including a re-issuance of the letter of credit to any successor to the landlord.

Attorneys also should bear in mind that if a letter of credit is payable upon presentation of a certificate signed by a named individual and that person dies, the issuing bank may not be required to pay the letter of credit. Samuel Rappaport Family Partnership v. Meridian Bank, 657 A. 2d 17 (Pa. Super. Ct. 1995).

LOST LETTERS OF CREDIT

Because the ISP does not require the issuer to replace a lost, stolen, mutilated or destroyed letter of credit (although it may do so at its discretion), the lease should contain a general cooperation provision requiring the tenant to take such actions as are reasonably necessary to ensure that the landlord is always fully secured with a letter of credit meeting the requirements of the lease, including any action reasonably necessary to effect the replacement of a lost, stolen, mutilated, or destroyed letter of credit.

TRANSFERABILITY

A letter of credit should specifically provide that it is transferable, so that the landlord can transfer the letter of credit to any person that buys or ground leases the building. Because the issuing bank charges a fee for transfer, either the lease should provide that the tenant pays the transfer fee as additional rent (although this is often a topic of negotiation) or the letter of credit should provide that it may be transferred without payment of any fee by the beneficiary.

The UCP, which governs many letters of credit, provides that a letter of credit may not be transferred more than one time unless it specifically states that it is transferable more than once. THIS IS A TRAP FOR THE UNWARY. Accordingly, the landlord=s attorney should ensure that any letter of credit subject to the UCP specifically provides that it is transferable one or more times. The ISP does not contain such a restriction. Accordingly, if a letter of credit governed by the ISP is "transferable," it may be transferred one or more times.

CONDITIONS TO PAYMENT OF LETTER OF CREDIT

A letter of credit is payable upon presentation to the issuing bank of the documents described in the letter of credit. If the documents presented diverge from the documents required by the letter of credit, the issuing bank may refuse to pay the letter of credit.

Accordingly, it is critically important that the letter of credit clearly describe the presentation documents. The simpler the required documentation, the better.

Accordingly, from the landlord's standpoint, the letter of credit should be payable upon presentation of the original letter of credit (although it is possible to draft a letter of credit to permit presentation of a copy of the letter of credit, the presentation of a copy increases the likelihood of a fraudulent presentation), together with a "sight draft" (which is like a check).

A copy of the required form of sight draft should be annexed to the lease agreement so there is no misunderstanding about the proper form of sight draft when presentation is made.. .

The tenant, on the other hand, will want the letter of credit to provide that the presentation documents include an affidavit to the bank that the tenant is in default of the lease beyond the applicable cure period.

This formulation carries 2 problems for the landlord: (a) cure periods usually commence on the delivery of notice, and a bankruptcy filing may prevent the landlord from giving notice (because of the operation of the automatic stay), and (b) the likelihood of litigation is increased.

Although the issuer is required by the ISP and UCP to pay the letter of credit upon delivery of the required affidavit and is not permitted to look behind the affidavit to determine the truth of the statements contained therein, the inclusion of such language is an invitation to litigation because it provides a ready target for the tenant, who will argue to a lower court judge, with little or no experience in letters of credit, that the draw on the letter of credit is fraudulent because one or more of the statements in the affidavit are untrue.

In such a situation, the landlord may very well lose the initial battle against the temporary restraining order, although it should ultimately win the fight.

Usually the landlord will agree, in the lease, that it will not present the letter of credit for payment unless tenant has defaulted under the lease and failed to cure a non-monetary default within the applicable cure period or tenant has failed to make any payment of rent or additional rent within a specified period.

If the tenant induces the landlord to agree to deliver to the bank a statement of some kind with its sight draft, the statement should be short and simple (e.g.The undersigned is drawing on the above-referenced Letter of Credit pursuant to a certain Lease, dated as of   , between   , as Owner, and , as Tenant, as said lease may have been amended, extended, and/or assigned@).

AUTOMATICALLY INCREASING AND DECREASING LETTERS OF CREDIT

If the tenant requests the landlord to decrease the amount of security upon an agreed date, and the landlord is willing to consent to such a reduction, the landlord's attorney should provide in the lease that the landlord will consent to an amendment of the letter of credit, upon the applicable date, to reduce the amount of security if certain agreed conditions are met (e.g., tenant is not in default of the lease beyond any applicable cure period, and tenant has made each payment of rent and additional rent within 10 days of the due date thereof).

The landlord should never agree to accept a letter of credit that provides for automatic reduction of the outstanding amount of the letter of credit, because the landlord could then be placed in a situation in which the letter of credit automatically reduces even if the tenant is then in default of the lease.

Occasionally the parties agree to fixed increases in security. For example, if a lease is signed 1 year before the space will be delivered, the tenant might wish to deliver to the landlord a letter of credit in an amount equal to half the security deposit upon signing of the lease, with provision for automatic increase in the security to the full amount on the date one year after issuance of the letter of credit. Letters of credit may provide for automatic adjustments in their outstanding amounts.

If the letter of credit is intended to automatically increase without further action by the bank, it should state that the increase will become effective "without amendment" or that the amendment will be "automatic." ISP §2.06.

LEASE PROVISIONS: Limiting Draw to Amount of Default.

The tenant may request the landlord to limit its draw down of the letter of credit to the amount by which tenant is in default. Landlord should resist. If there=s a non-payment default, landlord wants to be able to draw down the letter of credit in full and have the cash available to cover possible future defaults (it may decide to make a partial draw for bankruptcy reasons, but it is best to have the option to make a full draw).

Notice to Tenant. From the landlord=s perspective, the lease SHOULD NOT, as a condition to landlord=s draw down on a letter of credit, require the landlord to give the Tenant prior notice. If notice is required and the tenant files for bankruptcy before the applicable notice is given, the landlord will be unable to give the necessary notice by reason of the operation of the automatic stay.

One possible way of dealing with the notice issue is to provide that the landlord may draw on the letter of credit (a) if tenant defaults with respect to any of the terms, conditions or provisions of the lease on tenant's part to be observed or performed and such default continues beyond any applicable notice and cure period or (b) if tenant defaults with respect to any of the terms, conditions or provisions of the lease on tenant's part to be observed or performed and the transmittal of a notice of default is barred or stayed by applicable law. It is not clear whether such a formulation will work in the context of a tenant bankruptcy.

General Cooperation Clause. The lease should include a general savings clause that requires the tenant to cooperate with the landlord to effect any modifications, transfers or replacements of the letter of credit requested by landlord, so as to assure the landlord that it is at all times fully secured by a valid letter of credit that may be drawn upon by the landlord, its grantees, successors, representatives, and assigns.

Recovery of Attorneys' Fees. If the lease does not contain a general attorneys' fee provision broad enough to cover litigation involving the letter of credit, the lease provision dealing with letters of credit should provide for recovery of attorneys' fees if tenant seeks to enjoin payment of the letter of credit.

CONCLUSION

Letters of credit have bankruptcy advantages, but carry with them certain logistical disadvantages. Accordingly, the use of a letter of credit should be thoroughly discussed by the landlord and its attorney and the attorneys involved in the transaction should have a basic understanding of letters of credit.

LETTER OF CREDIT PROVISION – MANDATORY

(A) Concurrently with the execution of this Lease, Tenant shall deliver to Landlord a letter of credit meeting the requirements of this Article in the sum of $_____ (the "LC Amount").

Landlord may draw on the Letter of Credit (hereinafter defined) in whole or in part and use, apply, or retain the whole or any part of such proceeds, as the case may be, to the extent required for the payment of any rent, additional rent, damages, or any other sum payable by Tenant under this Lease, including but not limited to attorneys' fees for which Landlord is entitled to reimbursement pursuant to this Lease, re-letting expenses, and/or any rent and/or additional rent deficiency payable by Tenant, if (i) Tenant defaults in observing or performing any of the terms, provisions or conditions of this Lease on Tenant's part to be observed or performed, or (ii) Tenant, or any person or entity holding possession of the Premises through Tenant, holds over in possession of the Premises after the Expiration Date, or (iii) the Bank (hereinafter defined) sends a Non-Renewal Notice (hereinafter defined) as hereinafter provided.

If Landlord draws on the Letter of Credit, Tenant shall, within five (5) days after demand by Landlord, deliver to Landlord an additional Letter of Credit meeting the requirements of this Article or amend the existing Letter of Credit so that, at all times, the amount of the Letter of Credit held by Landlord, together with any cash held by Landlord not yet applied to any default by Tenant, equals the LC Amount.

If Tenant shall fully and faithfully comply with all of the terms, provisions, covenants and conditions of this Lease, and delivers possession of the Premises to Landlord at the Expiration Date in the condition required by this Lease, the Letter of Credit and any cash proceeds held by Landlord not applied pursuant to this Article, shall be returned to Tenant within 90 after the Expiration Date.

Such letter of credit (which letter of credit and any amended, additional, and/or replacement letter of credit received by Landlord that meets the requirements of this Article are hereinafter referred to collectively as a "Letter of Credit") shall name Landlord as beneficiary, shall be in the amount required by this Article, shall be issued by a commercial bank (the "Bank"), with offices for banking purposes in the City of New York, acceptable to Landlord, and shall be in form and substance satisfactory to Landlord.

Such Letter of Credit shall have an initial term of not less than one year, but shall automatically renew without amendment for consecutive periods of 1 year unless the Bank gives Landlord notice of non-renewal (a "Non-Renewal Notice") by certified or registered mail, return receipt requested, at least 60 days before the then expiration date of the Letter of Credit. The final expiration date of such Letter of Credit shall be at least ninety (90) days following the stated Expiration Date of this Lease.

Such Letter of Credit shall be clean, irrevocable, transferable one or more times without payment of any fee by the beneficiary, and payable in whole or partial drawings. The Letter of Credit shall be payable upon presentation of the Letter of Credit and a sight draft, with a form of the required sight draft annexed to such Letter of Credit.

If Landlord, at any time or from time to time, reasonably requests an amendment of the Letter of Credit (for example, to change the Landlord's address for notices or to change the identity of the Landlord beneficiary to reflect a merger or other change in the identity of Landlord), Tenant promptly shall cause the Letter of Credit to be so amended.

If the Letter of Credit is lost, stolen, or mutilated, Tenant shall cooperate with Landlord, promptly upon Landlord's request, to replace such Letter of Credit.

(C) If a Non-Renewal Notice is sent to Landlord, Landlord may draw on the Letter of Credit in whole or in part unless Tenant replaces the Letter of Credit with a substitute Letter of Credit meeting the criteria of this Article at least thirty (30) days prior to then expiration date of the Letter of Credit. Any proceeds held by Landlord may be applied as provided in Subpar. (A) above and/or may be used by Landlord to obtain a replacement Letter of Credit.

(D) Landlord (including any future Landlord) may transfer the Letter of Credit to any purchaser of the Building or any lessee to which Landlord leases the entire Building or any part thereof that includes the Demised Premises or any entity to which Landlord transfers its estate as tenant under any ground or underlying Lease, and the transferring Landlord shall thereupon be released by Tenant from all liability for the return of such Letter of Credit and any proceeds thereof. In such event, Tenant agrees to look solely to the new Landlord for the return of said cash proceeds or Letter of Credit.

(E) Landlord's use of the Letter of Credit proceeds shall not be deemed a waiver of Tenant's default or a waiver of any other rights and remedies to which Landlord may be entitled under the provisions of this Lease or any guaranty of this Lease by reason of such default, it being intended that Landlord's rights to use the whole or any part of the Letter of Credit proceeds shall be in addition to, but not in limitation of, any such other rights and remedies; and Landlord may exercise any of such other rights and remedies independent of or in conjunction with its rights under this Article.

Investing in real estate continues to be one of the best ways to build wealth and cut taxes. Benefits include the ability to recover the cost of income-producing property through depreciation, to use 1031 exchanges to defer profits from real estate investments, and to borrow against real estate equity to make additional investments or for other purposes.

Additionally, homeowners can benefit from the personal-residence exemption, which shields profits on the sale of a personal residence from capital gains taxes, as well as the deduction for mortgage interest. Read on to find out whether one or a combination of these strategies is right for you. KEY TAKEAWAYS

- ❖ Investing in real estate is a way to build wealth and reduce taxes through a variety of means.

- ❖ Depreciation allows for the recovery of costs related to income-producing rental property.

- ❖ Investors can defer taxes by selling an investment property and using the equity to purchase another property in what is known as a 1031 like-kind exchange.

- ❖ Property owners can borrow against the home equity in their current property to make other investments.

- ❖ Depending on the property sale value, home-owners can be excluded from capital gains taxes on the gains of their home sale.

- ❖ Individuals are also able to deduct the interest paid on their mortgages.

1. Using Depreciation Deduction

You can recover the cost of income-producing rental property through annual tax deductions called depreciation. The Internal Revenue Code defines the depreciation deduction as a reasonable allowance for deterioration, wear and tear, and a reasonable allowance for obsolescence.1

Real estate investors generally use a depreciation method called the Modified Accelerated Cost Recovery System (MACRS), in which residential rental property and structural improvements are depreciated over 27.5 years, while appliances and other fixtures are depreciated over 15 years.

Depreciation expense often results in a net loss on investment property even if the property actually produces a positive cash flow. This loss, as well as expenses, such as utilities and insurance, are reported on Schedule E, federal income tax Form 1040, and deducted from ordinary income.

2. Taking Advantage of 1031 Exchanges

The 1031 exchange, named for Section 1031 of the Internal Revenue Code, allows investors to defer taxes by selling one investment property and using the equity to purchase another property or properties of equal or greater value. This exchange must occur within a specified period of time.

Although a 1031 exchange can broadly include various types of property, the vast majority of transactions relate to real estate. And from Dec. 31, 2017, onward, Section 1031 "like-kind exchange treatment applies only to exchanges of real property held for use in a trade or business or for investment, other than real property held primarily for sale."3 □

Property Regulations

In order to successfully complete a 1031 exchange, the properties must meet the following criteria:

❖ The aggregate value of the replacement properties must be equal to or greater than that of the relinquished properties.

❖ The properties included in the transaction must be like-kind, meaning real property cannot be exchanged for some other type of asset, such as a real estate investment trust (REIT).

❖ Both properties must be held for "productive purposes in business or trade" (an investment).

Any cash or property received through the transaction that is not considered like-kind property is considered boot and is subject to taxation. Cash boot includes not only cash but also physical property, such as fixtures. Mortgage boot refers to any debt reduction that is achieved through the transaction.

Thus, the amount of debt assumed with the replacement property must be equal to or greater than the value of the debt retired when the relinquished property is sold.6☐

Investor Regulations

The investor must use a qualified intermediary. A qualified intermediary is an agent who facilitates the 1031 exchange process, largely by holding net proceeds from the relinquished property before they are re-invested in the replacement property. Only a qualified intermediary may hold those funds during the exchange. The Federation of Exchange Accommodators details the role that the qualified intermediary plays in the 1031 exchange process.

The investor is subject to two deadlines:

❖ Forty-five days after the sale of the relinquished property they must deliver a written list of the qualified replacement property to a qualified party to the exchange, usually the intermediary. There are also several rules that limit the number of properties that can be identified.

❖ Additionally, they must purchase the aggregate value of qualifying replacement assets within 180 days of selling the relinquished asset or 180 days after the due date of his tax return for that year, whichever occurs first.

1031 Exchange, Step by Step

In a typical transaction, an investor decides to sell an investment property and invest the proceeds from any gain in another property.

❖ To accomplish this in a tax-efficient way, the investor enters into a 1031 exchange agreement with a qualified intermediary and puts the original property up for sale.

At the same time, the investor begins searching for replacement properties.

❖ On the day the investor sells the original property (the relinquished property), the net proceeds after paying all expenses are sent to a special account set up by the qualified intermediary.

❖ The investor then enters into the identification period and has exactly 45 days to produce a list of qualified replacement properties and 180 days to close on the replacement property during the exchange period.

❖ Using the entire proceeds from the sale of the relinquished property, the investor closes on the new investment property or properties.

❖ The qualified intermediary wires those funds to the title company, the special account is closed and the transaction is completed.

3. Borrowing Against Home Equity

Investors who have built up sizable equity in either their personal home or investment property may simply choose to refinance their properties and pull out equity to make additional investments, improve the home, or for other purposes. Regulations vary from state to state.

In a typical scenario, a lender will loan 80% to 85% of your equity. For instance, on a $240,000 property with a $100,000 loan, the most a borrower could extract is $112,000 ($240,000 - $100,000) x 0.80 = $112,000).9

The ability to borrow against your equity will also depend on your credit score, your existing debt-to-equity ratio, and your debt-to-income ratio.

While this strategy is a bit riskier, for those able to handle the additional debt, it can help build wealth without having to enter into a 1031 exchange or sell a property.

4. Deferring Taxes on the Sale of a Home

Gains from the sale of a taxpayer's primary personal residence are excluded from capital gains taxation up to $500,000 for married couples that file jointly and $250,000 for single individuals if the taxpayer has lived in the home for two of the last five years. In addition, should the gains from the sale of a taxpayer's primary residence be greater than those exclusions, the taxpayer may also invest that portion through a 1031 exchange.

Investors who live in areas where home values are appreciating can use a strategy of trading up to both build their personal wealth and minimize taxes at the same time.

5. Deducting Mortgage Interest

Homeowners can deduct the portion of their mortgages attributable to interest payments on their tax returns. These payments are higher during the early years of the mortgage and gradually decrease as the mortgage is paid off.

According to the IRS, "you can deduct home mortgage interest on the first $750,000 ($375,000 if married filing separately) of indebtedness. However, higher limitations ($1 million ($500,000 if married filing separately)) apply if you are deducting mortgage interest from indebtedness incurred before December 16, 2017."11

The Bottom Line

There are many options available to the real estate owner who is looking to sell while minimizing tax liability.

- A 1031 exchange allows the returns from a sale to be reinvested into a like-kind property.

- A home equity loan taps directly into the value of the property and can be used for a variety of purposes.

- The sale of a principal residence is eligible for special tax treatment.

- Mortgage interest can be deducted at tax time.

Your personal situation will dictate which of these options is right for you, but any of them will help you get the most out of your real estate investment.

Chapter 10:

Revolving Credit Loans, Merchant Loans, And Installment Lines

Revolving credit is a credit line that remains available even as you pay the balance. Borrowers can access credit up to a certain amount and then have ongoing access to that amount of credit. They can repay the balance in full, or make regular payments. Each payment, minus the interest and fees charged, opens the credit again to the account holder.

Examples of revolving credit include credit cards, lines of credit, and home equity lines of credit (HELOCs). They work differently than installment loans. Learn about the pros and cons of a revolving line of credit.

KEY TAKEAWAYS

❖ Revolving credit is a line of credit that remains open even as you make payments.

❖ You can access money up to a preset amount, known as the credit limit.

❖ When you pay down a balance on the revolving credit, that money is once again available for use, minus the interest charges and any fees.

❖ You will pay interest on any balance carried over.

❖ Revolving lines of credit can be secured or unsecured.

How Does Revolving Credit Work?

When a borrower is approved for revolving credit, the bank or financial institution establishes a credit limit that can be used over and over again, all or in part. A credit limit is the maximum amount of money a financial institution is willing to extend to a customer seeking funds.

Revolving credit is generally approved with no date of expiration. The bank will allow the agreement to continue as long as the account remains in good standing. Over time, the bank may raise the credit limit to encourage its most dependable customers to spend more.Borrowers pay interest monthly on the current balance owed. Because of the convenience and flexibility of revolving credit, a higher interest rate typically is charged on it compared to traditional installment loans. Revolving credit can come with variable interest rates that may be adjusted. The costs of revolving credit vary widely:

- ❖ A home equity line of credit (HELOC) could be obtained with an interest rate slightly above mortgage rates. HELOCs are essentially second mortgages that use home equity as collateral.
- ❖ At the other end of the scale, credit cards come with average interest rates that are significantly higher. The average credit card interest rate was over 20% as of April 2023.2

Lenders consider several factors about a borrower's ability to pay before setting a credit limit. For an individual, the factors include credit score, current income, and employment stability. For an organization or company, the bank reviews the balance sheet, income statement, and cash flow statement.

Revolving Credit Examples

Common examples of revolving credit include credit cards, home equity lines of credit (HELOCs), and personal and business lines of credit. Credit cards are the best-known type of revolving credit. However, there are numerous differences between a revolving line of credit and a consumer or business credit card.

First, there is no physical card involved in using a line of credit as there is with a credit card. Lines of credit are typically accessed via checks issued by the lender.

Second, a line of credit does not require the customer to make a purchase. It allows money to be transferred into a customer's bank account for any reason without requiring an actual transaction using that money. This is similar to a cash advance on a credit card but does not typically come with the high fees and higher interest charges that a cash advance can trigger.

Types of Revolving Credit: Revolving credit can be secured or unsecured. There are major differences between the two. A secured line of credit is guaranteed by collateral, such as a home in the case of a HELOC. Unsecured revolving credit is not guaranteed by collateral, or an asset—for example, a credit card (unless it is a secured credit card, which does require the consumer to make a cash deposit as collateral.)

A company may have its revolving line of credit secured by company-owned assets. In this case, the total credit extended to the customer may be capped at a certain percentage of the secured asset. For example, a financial institution may set a credit limit at 80% of a company's inventory balance. If the company defaults on its obligation to repay the debt, the financial institution can foreclose on the secured assets and sell them to pay off the debt.

Because unsecured credit is riskier for lenders, it typically has higher interest rates.

Advantages and Disadvantages of Revolving Credit

The main advantage of revolving credit is that it allows borrowers the flexibility to access money when they need it. Many businesses small and large depend on revolving credit to keep their access to cash steady through seasonal fluctuations in their costs and sales.

As with consumers, rates for business lines of credit vary widely depending on the credit history of the business and whether the line of credit is secured with collateral. And like consumers, businesses can keep their borrowing costs minimal by paying down their balances to zero every month.

Revolving credit can be a risky way to borrow if not managed prudently. A significant part of your credit score (30%) is your credit utilization rate. A high credit utilization rate can have a negative impact on your credit score. Most credit experts recommend keeping this rate at 30% or below.

Revolving Credit vs. Installment Loan

Revolving credit differs from an installment loan, which requires a fixed number of payments including interest over a set period of time. Revolving credit requires only a minimum payment plus any fees and interest charges, with the minimum payment based on the current balance.

Revolving credit is a good indicator of credit risk and has the potential to impact an individual's credit score considerably. Installment loans, on the other hand, can be viewed more favorably on an individual's credit report, assuming all payments are made on time.

Revolving credit implies that a business or individual is pre-approved for a loan. A new loan application and credit reevaluation do not need to be completed for each instance of using the revolving credit.

Also, revolving credit is intended for shorter-term and smaller loans. For larger loans, financial institutions require more structure, including installment payments in preset amounts.

Is It Good to Have Revolving Credit?

Revolving credit is good to have in many cases, such as when you need access to funds and you want to pay them back over time. But, if not used responsibly, revolving credit could cause financial strain.

What Is a Good Amount of Revolving Credit to Have?

A good amount of revolving credit to have to best help your credit score is below 30% of your available credit. If you spend more than 30% of your available credit, your credit score will likely decline. Generally, the lower your credit utilization ratio, or the proportion of your balance to available credit, the better your credit score.

How Can Revolving Credit Help Your Credit Score?

Revolving credit can boost your credit score if you use it responsibly. To get the most out of revolving credit, make your minimum payments on time. Try to make more than the minimum payment or pay off your balances in full each month to avoid interest charges. And aim to keep your credit utilization ratio below 30%.

The Bottom Line

Revolving credit is a credit line that can be a valuable financial tool to help you pay for things. If you use revolving credit responsibly, you can build your credit score and potentially enjoy rewards like cash back or travel points. If you have a revolving credit line, be sure you make minimum payments on time, or your credit score could suffer.

Merchant loans are short-term business loans on which security is provided by way of your income from debit and credit card sales.

They work like this:

The lender advances an amount of cash backed by your predicted takings from your card machine or machines;

- ❖ You repay the lender each month according to an agreed percentage of your card machine income;
- ❖ Those repayments are made until the balance of the initial loan, plus the

lender's commission and charges, are repaid;

❖ This is typically calculated to last for around six months, but of course depends on the amount initially advanced, the income you actually receive from card sales, and the percentage of the loan you repay each month.

The precise amount of the initial advance and the fixed rate of the lender's commission and charges mean that you know the exact cost of such borrowing – and this may be factored into your cash flow budget.

Business finance through merchant loans

Different merchant loan providers have different limits on the amount you may borrow in this way – the government website, for example, suggests that it might be as much as £300,000, but this is likely to vary considerably from one merchant lender to another.

Clearly, you need to have been trading and using your card machines for some time – say, a year or more – so that the lender may base any advance on the anticipated debit and credit card sales. It may be, for instance, that the lender takes an average of your card income over the past six months.

You must also agree with the lender the percentage split – the percentage of your card machine takings that you repay each month to clear the initial loan. Typical percentages are between 10% and 30%. In other words, if your takings amount to £30,000 and you agreed a 20% split, you repay £6,000 each month until the loan is repaid.

The advantages

For businesses that rely heavily on card sales – such as retail and leisure industries – merchant loans have the advantage of your being able to repay the borrowing in line with the income you actually receive from your trading activities and card sales. If your income is high for the month, the percentage split means that you repay more – and may, therefore, clear your debt to the merchant lender more quickly.

If takings are down, however, you do not need to find so much to repay the lender.

This is in contrast to a standard fixed-rate, unsecured business loan, of course, where you need to find the same instalment to repay each month, regardless of sales and the actual performance of your business.

By the same token, however, there may be times when you may welcome the greater certainty of a standard business loan and the ease of budgeting for both your cash flow and working capital balance that is ensured by repaying a fixed amount each month.

Chapter 11:
Be Your Own Bank

5 Steps to Be Your Own Bank with Whole Life Insurance

Becoming your own banker may seem like smoke & mirrors, but when this private family banking concept is implemented correctly, you actually can recoup cash flows that would normally be lost forever while safely channel a massive amount of compounding in your favor.

The most popular private banking bestsellers (in bullets below) echo this bold claim, but they don't really elaborate in detail on the necessary steps to become your own banker:

❖ Becoming Your Own Banker – The Infinite Banking Concept * by Nelson Nash
❖ Bank on Yourself ** by Pamela Yellen (see footnotes for trademark details)

Upon first hearing that you can "be your own bank" you may have thought that you'd be starting a local bank branch in your neighborhood.

By now though you probably realize these books discuss borrowing against some sort of magical life insurance policy to double dip on growth when becoming your own banker.

Now you're probably left wondering if this whole "be your own bank" concept is a scam or legit, right?

I can personally attest to the fact that when executed correctly, borrowing against a properly-structured life insurance policy as your own bank can produce vastly more liquid wealth than if you saved and paid cash for everything in your life simply because of a very powerful mathematical force called compounding.

Wait... What?

Here are the most common ways people access whole life loans to become your own banker:

- ❖ Cars & Trucks
- ❖ College Tuition
- ❖ Real Estate (personal or investment)
- ❖ Business Inventory
- ❖ Business Equipment
- ❖ Major household expenses

Yes, there is actually merit to the underlying mechanics of this so-called "private family banking strategy" at the heart of these wordy books promoting "The Infinite Banking Concept®" * and "Bank on Yourself®." **

However, I will boil down this private family banking concept much more succinctly in 5 simple steps below.

The 5 Steps to Becoming Your Own Banker with Whole Life Insurance

Step 1 – Start a Whole Life Policy to Be Your Own Private Family Bank

Quite simply, the strategy requires that you take out a whole life insurance policy on yourself if you can qualify medically for it. If not, you can purchase a policy on someone close to you to be your own bank.

Warning: Insurance companies hate STOLI (stranger-owned-life-insurance) and so does the IRS.

However, here are the types of relationships insurance companies will sometimes issue a whole life policy on for you to own and control as your own bank:

- ❖ Spouse
- ❖ Child
- ❖ Business Partner
- ❖ Key employee
- ❖ People you have loaned significant amounts of money to

Note: With proper documentation, other scenarios may be possible to become your own banker using other people as the insured for your infinite banking life insurance.

Once you have identified who to buy insurance on, what's the next step?

Step 2 – Whole Life Policy Design Necessities and Add-ons to Become Your Own Banker

Now you shouldn't get any type of life insurance policy as your private family bank.

Nelson Nash's book "The Infinite Banking Concept – Becoming Your Own Banker" and Pamela Yellen's "Bank on Yourself" books insist that it must be a Participating Whole Life Insurance Policy from a mutual insurance company.

Although we are big fans of using certain Whole Life insurance policies for the infinite banking concept, we also recognize that certain Indexed Universal Life insurance (IUL policies) may also work if structured properly. However, since there is additional risk associated with these types of policies, we recommend that you fully understand all the pros and cons of Indexed Universal Life before using IUL to be your own bank.

Getting back to using the time-tested & true Whole Life insurance to become your own banker, we fully agree that it's of utmost importance to get your policy from a Mutual Life Insurance Company (as opposed to a stock insurance company). This is critical since mutual companies are owned by policyholders and share their profits with Whole Life policyholders in the form of dividends. It's what makes Whole Life insurance cash value a true non-correlated asset with solid steady growth rates, unlike "high-yield" savings accounts or CDs.

In order to maximize cash value growth and early access to the equity inside your own bank, you also will need to make sure your Whole Life policy includes these 2 key riders:

1. Paid-Up Additions (PUA) Rider: this is how to turbo-charge your "banking engine." (more on this below)\
2. Term Insurance Rider: this would be like the titanium frame that holds the turbo-charged engine in place.

FAQ: "But wait, a term insurance rider? I thought you needed Whole Life for IBC banking?"

Answer: When becoming your own banker, you do need Whole Life. However, blending it with this additional term rider can substantially bring down the overall cost of the total death benefit needed to support over funding. It also increases the amount of Paid-Up Additions you can buy in the early years, which is like the turbocharger that will greatly accelerate ongoing growth inside the whole life policy as your own bank.

Now that you know who to buy insurance on, where to buy it from, and which features you want to add, what's the next step to be your own bank?

Step 3 – Properly Funding Your Policy So You Can Become Your Own Banker

Now I realize that it seems completely counter intuitive to pay any more than you absolutely need to pay when it comes to insurance. So, prepare to have your paradigm shifted and your mind blown!

The way to outrun the internal costs of a Whole Life policy is to pay additional premium over and above the amount required for the basic coverage. In fact, you will want to pay substantially more when becoming your own banker... as much premium as the IRS will let you.

[Hint: When the IRS regulates anything, doesn't that usually mean that they're trying to limit something good going on there?]

Here are the 4 reasons you want to pay the maximum amount of Whole Life insurance premium to be your own bank:

1. The commission paid to the agent for the additional over funding payments is peanuts
2. 90-95% of this additional premium goes straight to your cash surrender value (in other words these over funding payments become immediately accessible inside your private family bank)
3. The other 5%-10% of this extra payment which doesn't go toward building immediate equity goes to buying a little slice of extra permanent death benefit (called a **Paid-Up Addition or PUA**). What's nice is that no further premiums will be due on PUAs since it is contractually paid-up with this one-time payment, hence the term Paid-Up Addition. PUAs immediately increase your Whole Life policy's guaranteed cash value as well as entitle you to a bigger cut of future dividend pools from your mutual insurance company.
4. These Paid-Up Additions get stacked onto your cash value which contractually starts growing at a favorable guaranteed rate of return (even if no dividends were ever paid again).

Now that you've got your banking engine in place, you've filled it with fuel, and the engine is humming, now what...?

Step 4 – Use Cash Value to Be Your Own Bank and Fund Expenditures and Fuel Outside Investments

Using our car analogy, it's time to take your infinite banking life insurance policy for a ride. Most people don't want to accumulate wealth simply just to have an impressive set of ink dots on an annual statement. You want to become your own banker to buy things, build wealth, and invest for your retirement and legacy.

Now you can utilize the equity inside your own bank to do these things at any time for any reason using one of these 4 methods:

1. Withdraw your cash surrender value or...
2. Borrow against your cash surrender value using the guaranteed policy loan feature for maximum flexibility
3. Increase your total borrowing capacity by using outside financing without even having to pledge your policy (i.e.: 1.9% Auto Loan)

4. Pledge the policy as collateral to a Cash Value Line of Credit (CVLOC) program when you can often get a better rate than a policy loan (or for convenience when you own multiple policies).

Now I know that most of you just cringe and see RED when you hear the words BORROW and LOAN.

That said, even though you are technically borrowing funds when becoming your own banker, your entire cash value balance continues growing within your Whole Life insurance policy, including the amount you borrowed.

Hmmmm...

You see, some people mistakenly think they are "borrowing out" the cash value from the policy and "paying themselves back with interest." That's not true at all and is often used as a deceptive sales pitch.

Your cash value never actually leaves your Whole Life policy even when you take a loan and "borrow against" it. You see, the mutual insurance company is happy to give you a loan out of their general account because they're always holding your cash value as collateral and it's guaranteed to grow every year no matter what!

That's why it seems like you pay yourself back the interest.

Again, this is important:

None of your cash value ever leaves your Whole Life policy when you borrow! Your entire cash value balance continues to grow inside your banking life insurance policy INCLUDING the amount you borrowed.

Question: "What if I don't ever want to pay back the darn loan?"

Answer: "You don't have to, but you may want to. And you have the ultimate flexibility in how you do that."

Step 5 – Pay Down the Loan ON YOUR TERMS with your Own Private Family Bank

Thankfully, a Whole Life policy loan is a private loan between you and the insurance company, so it doesn't show up on any credit report. Also, since the mutual company is holding your growing cash value as collateral, there's no stringent payment structure in place with your own bank. Here are your options for repayment:

- ❖ Pay principal and interest on whatever schedule you want
- ❖ Make interest-only payments
- ❖ Pay nothing until you can make a balloon payment for the entire balance Pay nothing (hoping the cash value growth keeps pace with the loan interest that's rolling up into the loan balance) then eventually have the Whole Life death benefit pay off the loan when the insured passes.

Needless to say, there's no other institution (or even a mafia loan shark) that offers this kind of flexibility to be your own bank with. Obviously, you should schedule some sort of regular loan maintenance, but it's certainly not required by the insurance company.

In fact, I have contractor clients who bid on jobs and have to come out of pocket for materials and labor costs. They float a Whole Life policy loan for close to a year and then pay it off in one fell swoop when they get paid for the entire job.

We encourage them to pay whatever minimum interest maintenance is needed to maintain simple interest on a flat loan balance while earning compound interest on an increasing cash value balance. However, when a banking life insurance policy is performing well as your own bank, the minimum required loan payment may be nothing at all

A lot of people hear how about paying interest on the loan and think, "Ah see, I knew there was a catch! I knew it was too good to be true."

But think about it – even if you just kept your cash in a bank account and made a withdrawal for every single purchase, don't you start making deposits shortly thereafter to true up the account for the next purchase?

So if you apply the exact same "save-spend-replenish" routine but instead funnel the exact same cash flows through a properly designed Whole Life insurance policy as your own private family bank, you will often see that the difference in net wealth is staggering when practicing what they call the **infinite banking concept.**

Here are the 3 reasons why becoming your own banker using life insurance works:

1. Your cash value usually earns a much better growth rate than any bank account, CD, or even safe bonds (with minimal fluctuating values)
2. The growth, as well as any lifetime distributions, are immune from income tax as long as some small amount of whole life insurance death benefit stays in place until the insured passes away.
3. When you borrow rather than make a withdrawal, your full cash value continues growing inside the policy despite any loans you have against the policy with the insurance company.

That's it! And that third factor is huge. Believe it or not, the combination of these 3 factors can contribute to vastly more wealth for the policyholder if this banking strategy is employed properly.

What I mean by that is that you should pay your loans back as soon as you can so you can continue to practice the banking concept throughout your Whole Life.

Question: If you have a goose laying golden eggs, when would you want to kill the goose?

Answer: Never!!! In fact, feed that goose as early and as often as you can so it keeps laying more and more golden eggs.

Chapter 12:

Trust

When it comes to trusts, most people are familiar with individual trusts, trust funds or family trusts that are connected to an individual or family. But another type of trust exists for entrepreneurs and companies called business trusts, which are also known as common law trusts. A business trust is a legal instrument that can be used to delegate the authority to manage a beneficiary stake in a certain business. It can also be used to run the business itself. However, there are multiple types of business trusts, with each working slightly differently. If you're thinking of using a business trust, it might be a good idea to consult with a financial advisor.

Functionally, a business trust is quite similar to an individual or family trust. It helps delegate control of assets to a trustee, who manages the trust and its contents on behalf of the grantor. An individual trust typically contains assets such as money or property, but a business trust holds the rights to an individual's stake or interest in a business. As a result, a business trust can be the legal entity that technically owns a business.

Business trusts can have one or multiple beneficiaries. A business can be owned by multiple trusts and entities or just a single one. They are primarily used to safeguard against taxes and liability, as trusts tend to have different legal protections than individuals. However, the specifics of these rules can vary by state.

A business **trust is a legal agreement.** In turn, the process of creating one typically begins with a conversation between the involved parties and a trust lawyer who can help define the terms of the agreement. Following this, the trust is legally created through what is called a declaration of trust.

The declaration of trust details the terms of the trust and delegates instructions and responsibilities for the trustee. These may include the valid length of the trust and the duties, powers and interests of the beneficiaries. Once the terms are settled, the one who owns the trust signs the declaration, officially creating it in the process.

The trustee of a business trust has a fiduciary duty to act in the best interests of the beneficiaries of the trust.

This is the same kind of fiduciary duty that applies to other financial situations. Most notably, SEC-registered financial advisors have a fiduciary duty to act in the best interests of their clients.

The trustee is the one who holds the rights and control of the business stake in the trust. It's typically one individual serving as a trustee of a business trust. At the end of the trust's length, the business interests transfer to its beneficiaries. Business trusts are treated as corporations and may conduct business transactions just like individuals.

Just as there are several different types of individual trusts, there are three main categories of business trusts. Here's a breakdown of each:

Grantor Trust

The first type is called a grantor trust. Grantor trusts consist of a grantor, a trustee and a beneficiary. This type of trust is very self-contained.

The grantor pays taxes on the income that comes from the trust and has complete control over it. This includes control over business distributions to the beneficiaries.

Simple Trust

Next is a simple trust. For a trust to fall into this category, its status must be verified by the IRS. With a simple trust, the trustee must distribute business profits directly to the beneficiaries. It's also prohibited from doing things like touching any principal assets.

Complex Trust

A complex trust is in some ways the opposite of a simple trust, though it still isn't managed by the beneficiaries of the trust. Business profits and other funds may be distributed only in part to beneficiaries and may even be contributed to other organizations, such as charities. In order to maintain status as a complex trust, the trust needs to have at least some form of income.

Financial trusts aren't a mandatory part of estate planning. However, they may help protect your assets and loved ones. They can also streamline the property distribution process after your death.

Establishing a trust makes it easier to transfer belongings to the people or organizations you choose, while reducing the tax burden they might face. Some trusts also shield your assets from probate, lawsuits, and the IRS.

And if you're thinking about setting up a trust, consider purchasing a life insurance policy to ensure your assets go to your loved ones. Life insurance benefits are typically disbursed tax-free, and your beneficiary can use the proceeds to pay estate taxes or other debts your estate may owe.

You also have the option to set up certain trusts using life insurance. For example, if you have a loved one with special needs, you might not have enough money to fund a special needs trust on your own. With life insurance, you can apply for a death benefit that will provide financial security for your beneficiary, such as your spouse, children, or a charitable organization.

Learning about your options can help you plan for your loved ones' future. Let's take a look at some of the most common types of trusts to consider during the estate planning process.

9 Different Types of Trusts for Estate Planning

Revocable trust

A revocable trust allows the grantor — the person who created the trust — to change or end the trust at any point during their lifetime. Revocable trusts are also known as living trusts or revocable living trusts.

These trusts are set up by you while you're still alive. Often, the assets in a living trust transfer to your beneficiaries after you pass away. Most trusts can be revocable.

Having a revocable trust in place can help you avoid probate, which is the process a court takes to finalize your legal and financial matters after your death. Probate can be lengthy and expensive for your loved ones. Estates in probate also become a matter of public record.

One downside of a revocable trust is that the assets held in one are considered personal assets to creditors and for estate tax purposes.

This means if you owe money when you pass away, creditors can access to your trust's assets to pay off those debts. You may also owe taxes on your estate if your assets meet the minimum value requirements.

Living trust vs. revocable trust: What's the difference?

Living trusts and revocable trusts are often used interchangeably, which can cause some confusion. But a living trust is simply another name for a revocable trust.

Like a revocable trust, a living trust is one you set up and manage during your lifetime. You can update or dissolve a living trust at any time. After you pass, the assets in a living trust are transferred to your beneficiaries.

Irrevocable trust

Once you create an irrevocable trust you cannot change or terminate it. You can establish an irrevocable trust during the estate planning process. Most trusts can be irrevocable.

An irrevocable trust offers your assets the most protection from creditors and lawsuits.

Assets in an irrevocable trust aren't considered personal property. This means they're not included when the IRS values your estate to determine if taxes are owed. And, if you file bankruptcy or default on a debt, assets in an irrevocable trust won't be included in bankruptcy or other court proceedings.

Pro tip: A revocable trust becomes irrevocable when you pass away. This allows you to change the trust's terms or update your beneficiaries while you're alive, guaranteeing your wishes are carried out. However, it doesn't prevent your estate from entering probate.

Testamentary trust

A testamentary trust is one you create through your will. Also known as a will trust or a trust under will, testamentary trusts don't activate until you pass away. Your last will and testament includes instructions on how your trust is created, managed, and distributed. It also ensures your beneficiaries only receive their inheritance at a certain time.

It's important to understand that assets in a testamentary trust always go through the probate process. As a result, your estate becomes a matter of public record, which means your beneficiaries will lose some of the privacy that comes with other types of trusts.

Special needs trust

If you have a disabled loved one(s), a special needs trust can provide them with income after your passing without disqualifying them from government benefits, like Social Security Disability Income.

Keep in mind that your special needs beneficiary doesn't control the funds. Instead, a trustee — or someone you choose to manage the trust — does.

Spendthrift trust

Spendthrift trusts distribute assets to your beneficiaries over time, rather than in a lump sum. Your beneficiaries receive payouts over a specified period, which can help ensure your savings last.

The funds in a spendthrift trust aren't considered your beneficiary's personal assets until they're disbursed. This means creditors can't access money in the trust in the case of loan default or bankruptcy.

Charitable trust

If you want to donate money in a tax-efficient manner when you pass away, a charitable trust may be a good option. Assets included in the trust aren't considered personal assets, so they won't be vulnerable to estate taxes.

You can typically choose from two types of charitable trusts: charitable lead trusts and charitable remainder trusts (CRT).

Charitable lead trusts allow you to set aside specific assets for one or more organizations. Then, you can distribute the rest of your property to your beneficiaries — like your spouse or children. Charitable lead trusts are irrevocable, which means you can't change the terms once they're established.

A charitable remainder trust is an irrevocable trust you can use as a source of income until your death. When you establish a CRT, you place assets into the trust, such as money, real estate, or stocks.

You can draw income from this funding source for the rest of your life. When you pass away, the remaining assets in your CRT will be distributed to one or more charitable organizations.

Asset protection trust

This type of trust keeps your assets safe from creditors. If you file bankruptcy or default on a debt, assets in this trust won't be included in bankruptcy or other court proceedings.

Asset protection trusts can be expensive to establish. However, they provide more security than any other type of trust — except for an irrevocable trust.

Bypass trust

A bypass trust is a popular option for married couples. This trust allows you to leave assets to your spouse estate-tax-free. Following the death of one spouse, the assets in a bypass trust are split into two parts: a revocable marital trust and an irrevocable family trust.

When the first spouse passes, their assets are placed in the family trust. The surviving spouse owns the marital trust, though they can receive income from the family trust during their lifetime.

Then, when the surviving spouse passes away, their assets go to their beneficiaries — again avoiding estate taxes and the probate process.

Totten trust

A Totten trust is essentially a payable-on-death (POD) bank account. It's a revocable trust that you can set up with your bank by simply filling out paperwork and naming a POD beneficiary. This helps you maintain control of the account during your life while avoiding probate after you've passed away.

Chapter 13:

Shell company

Shell companies came under the spotlight following the 2016 Panama Papers publication. The extent of their use for illegal or immoral purposes, largely for money laundering or tax avoidance, caused public outrage and a ripple of legislative changes around the world.

A Shell company is one that primarily or solely exits on paper only. This means that there will be no significant assets linked to the shell company and it will deliver no goods, services or other business functions to generate revenue for itself.

It will have no functional physical office and if it has a registered address this will most likely be a mailbox or an address that is shared by up to hundreds of other shell companies.

Primarily shell companies are used to move or hold assets in a manor where it is not immediately obvious who the ultimate beneficiary is. Shell companies can be set up by a third party, often a lawyer or accountant, to further obscure this; and a shell company is able to have any number of subsidiary shell companies under it.

Shell corporations can exist in any country but are very popular in those that are considered tax havens or have low regulatory standards; such as: The Cayman Islands, British Virgin Islands, Bermuda or The Channel Islands are examples of High Risk Countries.

Shell companies can be set up and used by legitimate businesses as well as criminal enterprises and can be used by individuals as well as organizations.

There are numerous reasons that legitimate companies would use a shell company and they very commonly do.

If a company wants to do business or invest in a foreign market, they may set up a shell company in that country so transactions take place within one regulatory space and are not complicated by going between borders and regulatory laws. In this case legitimate business would be done by individuals in the home country but it would be as if they operated out of the shell company in the second country.

Shell companies may be set up as a precursor to them becoming a fully operational business and may hold assets whilst they are being set up.

Companies operating in volatile economies can use shell companies to store money in more stable economies and possibly avoid paying tax.

An extremely popular use for shell companies by legitimate enterprises is tax and regulatory avoidance.

A common example of shell companies being used for UK tax avoidance is companies using shell companies in Ireland, which has a lower corporate tax rate than the UK, and attributing their profits from UK operations to this shell company; thus paying less tax.

Should a company wish to avoid the costs and impediments of complying to high standards of regulations they in some cases they can set up a shell company in a country that has lower standards to avoid these. For example, a UK company performing activities abroad may be held to certain environmental standards by UK regulations, they can set up a shell company in a suitably poorly regulated country and attribute the activities to this shell company in an effort to avoid tax law enforcement.

Shell corporations play a pivotal role in money laundering schemes, both in the washing of illicit funds and in obfuscating ownership of financial assets held in their name.

Money laundering has three distinct stages: placement, layering and integration.

❖ Placement – illegally gained cash is placed into the banking system. Turning the physical notes into digital money in a bank account.

❖ Layering – the money is then sent through a complex series of transactions, often crossing international borders, to hide the original source of the funds

❖ Integration – the money can no longer be easily attributed to illegal activity and is essentially clean. It can then be used as if it were legitimate funds

Shell businesses are integral to the layering stage of money laundering. The aim is to create a chain of as many transactions as possible, essentially to make it as confusing as possible for investigating authorities to trace the source or destination of funds.

These chains may contain dozens or even hundreds of shell companies across multiple countries.The advantage of money laundering schemes crossing international borders is that an authority investigating a money laundering scheme will only have jurisdiction in its own country and cross border collaboration between police forces slows or even halts investigations.

Also, the countries that are popular for laundered money to be routed through tend to have low or no financial regulations which would mean their authorities would not aid in the investigation as no crime had been committed on their soil.

Many such countries also have a vested interest in allowing these schemes to prosper as they collect tax on these funds whilst not having to provide anything in return, save their lack of regulations.

To add further complexity, shell companies will not be set up in the name of the ultimate owner of the illicit funds and frequently will be listed under a false name. Even in the UK it takes a matter of minutes to create a shell company attributed to a fake identity, which can be used for illegal transactions and then abandoned with little chance of ever being traced to who initially created it.

Shell companies are also used in the placement stage of money laundering schemes. Once the washed funds have made their way back to the destination economy, they can be stored anonymously in the accounts of shell companies or used to purchase assets, such as property and real estate, which are then held under said shell companies name.

As Shell companies are not illegal in and of themselves and do have legitimate uses business can be done with them in certain instances.

The Money Laundering, Terrorist Financing and Transfer of Funds (Information on the Payer) Regulations 2017 makes it a legal requirement for companies in the regulated sector to adopt a **risk-based approach** for all business dealings. This includes confirming who the ultimate beneficiary is for any given transaction.

Considering Shell companies do not conduct business activities for themselves there will always be an ultimate beneficiary to identify. This not being freely given is a recognized sign of illicit activity, as is a party seeking undue secrecy.

Should a shell company be easily linked to a legitimate company or individual, and all other anti-money laundering requirements be met, then it may be appropriate to do business with them.

Why Should I Be Concerned about Shell Companies?

Shell companies in and of themselves are legal and in many cases they are used for legitimate reasons. However, shell corporations are also commonly used as vessels for committing financial crimes, such as:

Money laundering

Money laundering is a form of financial crime that allows criminals to hide the profits of crime, or disguise the illicit sources of their wealth. Criminals do this by distributing money in such a way as to make it difficult to trace.

Shell corporations are useful tools for money launderers because they are easy to set up and their ownership can be difficult to determine.

Illegal Business

Shell companies can also be used by people who want to engage in illegal business without revealing their identity.

For example, a company or individual can use a shell company to fund terrorist activities without this funding being traced back to them.

Shell corporations can also be used to conceal one's identity when doing business with an unpopular client—for example, if a company wants to profit from a region or industry while giving the outward appearance of boycotting it to please the public.

Although this is not illegal, this kind of activity is misleading and likely to garner negative media attention if discovered.

Concealing assets

Shell companies are commonly used to conceal assets during divorces, court cases, mergers, or acquisitions.

People do this to avoid having to share their financial assets when they divorce, having their significant assets seized during litigation, or having them taken over during a corporate merger or acquisition.

Deliberately hiding assets in this way is a form of fraud, and is illegal.

Tax Evasion

Shell corporations are also frequently used by companies or high-earning individuals to avoid or evade tax.

Tax avoidance involves avoiding paying while obeying the letter of the law, while tax evasion is unlawful avoidance of tax. Shell companies are frequently used for both.

Shell corporations are frequently used to evade tax because they are relatively easy to set up and difficult to trace. One of the main ways people use shell companies for tax evasion is by hiding taxable income and financial assets in a shell corporation in a different country.

Certain countries are such popular locations for tax avoidance and evasion through shell companies that they are commonly referred to as tax havens, because they have low tax rates and little tax regulation.

The world's five most popular tax havens—measured by the amount of money they hold versus how much they should hold based on their local economies—are the British Virgin Islands, Taiwan, Jersey, Bermuda, and the Cayman Islands.

Chapter 14:

Start Your Business Using A.I

Validator.ai.com - use this website to get feedback on your business ideas.

Namingmagic.com - use this website to get a domain.

Logoai.com - To create a logo for your business.

Durable.co - To create a website.

Millet.ai - No need to hire photographers, just use this AI website.

Chapter 15:

$85k Jewelry Credit

Apply with the lenders below:

- ❖ Wells Fargo Jewelry Advantage - $50,000
- ❖ Klarna - $20,000
- ❖ Synchrony - $5,000
- ❖ Acima - $5,000
- ❖ Snap Finance - $5,000

www.ingramcontent.com/pod-product-compliance
Lightning Source LLC
Chambersburg PA
CBHW070010300526
45794CB00001B/269